First Steps in SAP®
Financial Accounting (FI)

Ann Cacciottoli

Ann Cacciottoli
First Steps in SAP® Financial Accounting (FI)

ISBN: 978-1-5148-5953-7

Editor: Tracey Duffy

Proofreading: Tracey Duffy

Cover Design: Philip Esch, Martin Munzel

Cover Photo: iStockphoto # 3356691 © Yuri

Interior Design: Johann-Christian Hanke

All rights reserved.

1st Edition 2015, Gleichen

© 2015 by Espresso Tutorials GmbH

URL: *www.espresso-tutorials.com*

Feedback
We greatly appreciate any kind of feedback you have concerning this book. Please mail us at *info@espresso-tutorials.com*.

Table of Contents

Preface

In 2001 I gladly accepted an offer to participate in an enterprise transformation project for a large paper-based packaging company.

The project turned out to be the catalyst for a welcome career change from being an accountant to becoming a technology professional and ultimately led to my current position as an SAP technology consultant with a top consulting firm.

Along the way, not only have I have experienced first-hand the challenges of learning new software applications, but I have also witnessed end users struggling to meet the expectations of their employers as new systems are installed.

Training for new software, when offered, may not be timely. It is often conducted months in advance of the end user's accessibility to the application. When the end user finally has access to the software, it is in a productive environment where there is no opportunity to practice new skill sets or explore functionality as the user may have done in their training environment.

Training by the software vendor may not be made available to all end users: training is expensive to deliver and many end users need to access only a limited number of specific functions. Therefore, incurring the cost of vendor-delivered training may not make sense for the company. In these instances, end user training will be developed in-house. It may consist of a step-by-step instruction document—just enough to get the job done, but lacking information about why certain steps should be performed. The instructions fail to provide the end user with insight into the impact of the data that is being entered.

In addition to frequently working with employees who need to transition to an SAP environment, I have often been asked in social settings "where can I learn SAP?". With the multitude of companies operating on SAP systems, these inquiries are generally from those who are considering seeking employment in an SAP accounting environment, or perhaps just looking to enhance their knowledge of the software. They do not want to spend the time or resources attending a class and are more likely to prefer a self-paced option.

How this book is organized

The intended audience for *Getting Started with SAP FI* is individuals new to SAP, or even new to an accounting environment, who are looking for quick, inexpensive, and stress-free learning that can immediately be put to use on the job or during a job interview. The publication:

1. Provides the beginner and/or casual user with an introduction to SAP FI

2. Provides simple instructions for recording basic financial transactions by executing common SAP transaction codes

3. Reinforces learning with illustrations

4. Provides the reader with the opportunity to practice at his or her own pace using an Internet Demonstration and Education System (IDES)

Rather than address SAP FI using the language of seasoned consultants or information technologists, the book presents concepts from a business user's perspective. The goal of the book is to enable the reader to confidently enter basic financial transactions and execute standard SAP reports from the SAP menus delivered in the IDES system.

Chapter 1 provides an overview of SAP Financials (FI) and describes how SAP FI is integrated with the rest of the SAP Enterprise Resource Planning (ERP) suite.

Chapters 2 to 4 are the central focus of *Getting Started with SAP FI*: these chapters focus on the modules General Ledger (GL), Accounts Receivable (AR), and Accounts Payable (AP). Each chapter first presents the master data objects that are necessary before transactions can be posted in an SAP system. The reader will learn how to display and create general ledger accounts, customers, and vendors. The chapters then provide instructions for several methods of entering transactions in the SAP system. Finally, many of the available reports are explored.

Chapter 5 provides the configuration settings which were used in the IDES environment when writing this book.

The chapters provide a step-by-step guide for entering transactions and can also serve as a future reference. The beginner to SAP should be able to quickly develop the minimal skills required for navigating in the

SAP FI application and become proficient in entering transactions and using SAP FI reports.

Throughout the book, exercises are recommended which the reader can perform in an SAP Internet Demonstration and Evaluation System (IDES) environment. It is assumed that the reader is familiar with logging on to the SAP system and can navigate using the SAP Easy Access menu, as well as execute SAP transaction codes by clicking the menu item or entering the transaction code in the command field.

Solutions to the exercises can be found in Appendix C on page 201.

We have added a few icons to highlight important information. These include:

Tip

 Tips highlight information concerning more details about the subject being described and/or additional background information.

Warning

 Warnings draw attention to information that you should be aware of when you go through the examples from this book on your own.

Finally, a note concerning the copyright: All screenshots printed in this book are the copyright of SAP SE. All rights are reserved by SAP SE. Copyright pertains to all SAP images in this publication. For simplification, we will not mention this specifically underneath every screenshot.

1 What is SAP FI?

This chapter introduces you to SAP. Using the Financial Accounting Easy Access menu as a guide, this chapter includes an overview of SAP FI and explains how to navigate to the most common transactions.

1.1 What is SAP?

SAP is a German software company that started in the early 1970s and has grown to be the largest business software company in the world. The main software product of SAP is known as ERP (Enterprise Resource Planning). ERP is a suite of software applications that can help companies manage all aspects of their business activities — from product manufacturing or service delivery to marketing and sales, and to accounting for reporting business results.

As the company has continued to grow and respond to enhancements in technology, so too has the suite of applications that the company offers. This book focuses on one of the core applications in SAP Business Suite: SAP Financials, referred to as SAP FI.

1.2 Introduction to accounting

Before delving into SAP FI, it may be helpful for some readers to have an explanation of some of the elementary aspects of accounting or bookkeeping without consideration of software. The principle purpose of accounting is to measure and report information about the activities of a business enterprise and also to provide a picture of its economic health. Modern day accounting dates as far back as the 1200s; however, it is often Luca Pacioli, a Franciscan friar and friend of Leonardo DaVinci, who is credited in the late 1400s with the first publication that defined *double-entry* accounting, a process which is used worldwide to the present day.

The term double-entry could be misconstrued by those outside the business world to mean that two sets of records are maintained. In reality, double-entry bookkeeping refers to the notion of equal and offsetting entries — a debit and a credit — which are used to record each and every business transaction. Business transactions are recorded in *accounts*. Accounts can be thought of as buckets that collect transactions so that they can be summarized for reporting and analysis. Think of a merchant who is recording cash received for a sale. The two-sided entry would be comprised of a debit entry in the bucket or account *Cash* and a credit to *Sales*. At the end of the day (or week, or month), the merchant can add up all of the entries in the *Sales* account to calculate the total revenue that has been realized. When the merchant has to pay for an expense, such as rent for his store, he would enter a credit amount in his *Cash* account and a debit amount in his *Rent Expense* account. When he then tallies up all of the entries in the cash account, he would have the total of his cash position. By subtracting the total debits in rent or other expense accounts from the sales revenue account, he would also have a picture of the profit he has realized from running his store.

This example is obviously quite simple. In reality, businesses maintain dozens of accounts and in a large corporation there may be hundreds of accounts. The number of accounts needed is dictated by the nature of the business and by legal and tax authority requirements.

The most basic premise of double-entry bookkeeping is the following *accounting formula*: assets – liabilities = owner's equity. At the end of any accounting period, the net of all entries in revenue and expense accounts is an increase (or decrease if expenses are greater than revenue) in owner's equity. The summation of the net increase or decrease in all of the revenue and expense accounts provides a picture of the results of the business activity. The summation of all assets minus liabilities provides a picture of the net worth of the business. The results of business activity are presented in a somewhat standard format known as a *profit & loss* or *P&L* report. The net worth of a business is presented in a report known as a *balance sheet*. There are other reports desired and required for a business enterprise but these two are the essence of financial reporting.

In order to facilitate the preparation of the P&L and balance sheet reports, every account in the business can be categorized as one of the following types of account: asset, liability, revenue, expense, or equity. It is worth repeating that every business transaction is comprised of at least one debit and one credit to one or more of the accounts.

1.3   Why SAP FI?

The sheer volume of activity in most businesses necessitates the use of software to record and summarize business transactions. SAP FI provides a perfect solution for managing this volume.

Of course, the legal and tax requirements are not the only reason that businesses capture and report transactional information. Businesses are interested in details of operations that will help them become more efficient and more profitable. They may be interested in comparing the costs of production across several plants to capitalize on the efficiencies of one particular plant. They may consider the profitability of certain products or customers when making business decisions about which products to produce or which customers to retain. The SAP ERP system is an integrated suite of applications of which SAP FI is only a small, but very important part. Other application areas include Controlling (management reporting), Materials Management (inventory control and product costing), Sales and Distribution, and Human Resources to name just a few. Because all of the other applications result in business transactions, SAP FI is a prerequisite for using any of the other applications.

1.4   SAP FI menu

Within the SAP FI application, there are also several modules, not all of which are covered in this book. Figure 1.1 shows the modules found under the FINANCIAL ACCOUNTING path of the SAP EASY ACCESS menu.

Figure 1.1: SAP Easy Access menu – SAP FI

Of the many modules listed, this book focuses on General Ledger, Accounts Receivable, and Accounts Payable. Each of these modules comes with transaction codes which you can execute to enter documents in the SAP system. For example, Figure 1.2 shows sections of the Accounts Payable menu expanded with the transaction codes listed to the left of the menu description. There are two ways to execute any transaction:

1. Expand the menu until the desired transaction appears and then double-click the desired transaction.

2. Enter the transaction code in the command field in the upper left corner of the SAP EASY ACCESS screen and select the ENTER icon (or press ⌈Enter⌋ on your keyboard).

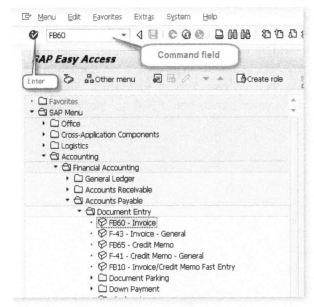

Figure 1.2: SAP Easy Access menu – Accounts Payable

What do I do if transaction codes are not displayed?

If transaction codes are not displayed, choose EXTRAS • SETTINGS from the toolbar and make sure that DISPLAY TECHNICAL NAMES is selected, as shown in Figure 1.3.

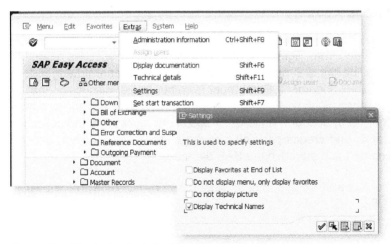

Figure 1.3: Displaying technical names (transaction codes)

13

Adding transactions to the Favorites folder

You can add transactions to your FAVORITES folder in the SAP Easy Access menu. Right-click a transaction in the menu and then choose ADD TO FAVORITES. Figure 1.4 illustrates adding transaction FB60 to the FAVORITES folder.

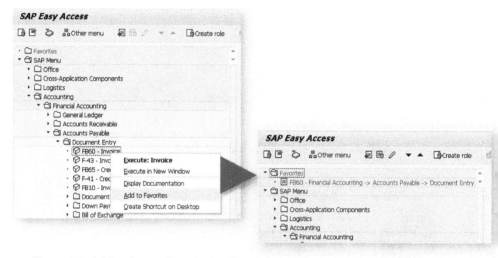

Figure 1.4: Adding transactions to the Favorites folder

1.5 SAP documents

As you can see from Figure 1.4, there are several transactions related to documents. Before we move on to the chapter on General Ledger, let's display an SAP document. Remember from our earlier discussion that all business transactions result in at least one debit and one credit to a general ledger (G/L) account. An SAP FI document represents the collection of the debits and credits pertaining to the business transaction that has been recorded and stored in the SAP database.

From the General Ledger menu, select FB03 – DISPLAY, as shown in Figure 1.5.

Figure 1.5: FB03 – Display

As shown in Figure 1.6, we select document number 1800000046 which has been created for demonstrating what an FI document looks like. After entering the document number, company code, and fiscal year, select the ENTER icon (✅) or press ⌨Enter on the keyboard to retrieve the document.

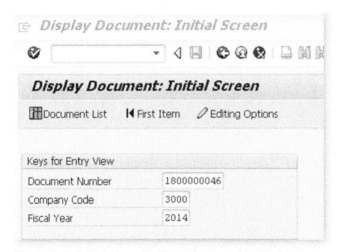

Figure 1.6: Criteria for selecting a document to display

The SAP system returns a view of the document as shown in Figure 1.7.

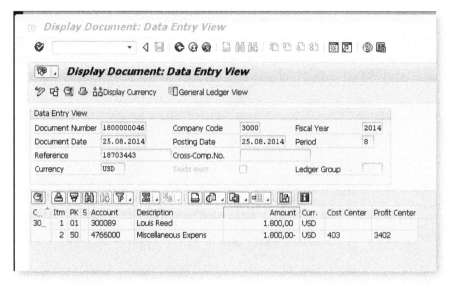

Figure 1.7: SAP document display

Note that there are two sections in the display. The top section represents the header information for the document and this information pertains to both the debit and credit parts of the document. The lower section represents the line item detail. We can see that there is one account
receiving a debit (in this case a customer account) and another account,
MISCELLANEOUS EXPENSE receiving a credit, as evidenced by the minus
sign after the amount.

We will look at document display further in Chapter 3.

1.6 Exercises

Solutions to the exercises can be found in Appendix C on page 201.

1.6.1 Log in to the IDES client, expand the menu, and answer the following questions

1. List three transaction codes for entering a General Ledger (G/L) account document.

2. List three transaction codes for entering an Accounts Payable (AP) document.

3. List three transaction codes for entering an Accounts Receivable (AR) document.

1.6.2 Add transaction FB03 – Display (document) to the Favorites folder

1.6.3 Navigate to the Enter G/L Account Document screen and exit without creating an entry

How do I exit a transaction without saving?

To exit a transaction without saving the information entered, hover over the icons in the toolbar to display their texts and then select the EXIT icon.

2 Getting started with SAP General Ledger

Before posting transactions to the general ledger in an SAP system, you must first understand the master data that is required in order for postings to be processed. This chapter includes a discussion of master data as compared with transaction data. You will learn how to create or simply view master data. The chapter also describes and compares SAP's *Classic GL* with *New GL*. Finally, the chapter introduces many of the transaction codes that enable you to enter actual postings.

2.1 What is FI master data?

One fine morning I arrive at my local bank to deposit a check that I have received. Unfortunately, I have not remembered to bring a deposit slip, nor can I remember my account number. The teller must log into the bank system and find my account number. The record in the bank system that contains my name, address, other personal information, and my account number is known as *master data*. The master data represents (relatively) static information about me, but does not in any way reflect activity that has occurred or will occur in my account. When the teller processes my deposit, additional data is recorded in the bank system — *transaction data*. Without my master data, the deposit transaction could not be entered in the bank system. However, my master data may exist in the bank system for any period of time, even if there are never any transactions entered. Therefore, you can think of master data as descriptive information and of transaction data as activity information.

Many master data objects are required to post a general ledger transaction depending on the specific configuration of the SAP environment; the most common object required is a general ledger (or G/L) account.

2.1.1   G/L accounts

Section 1.2 introduced the concept of an *account*. Looking at types of accounts in more detail, a general ledger (or G/L) account is an excellent example of master data specifically related to the general ledger. A general ledger account must exist before transactions can be recorded. When a general ledger transaction is recorded, it includes a general ledger account number and an amount. The nature of the account is not included in the transaction record; instead, this information is included in a general ledger *master file* which contains a list of general ledger account numbers and descriptions.

You can think of a master file as a collection of index cards. Each card details the account number and a description of the account. Of course, in the SAP system, there are no physical index cards; instead, the cards or records are contained in data files. The master file record also contains other attributes for the account. For example, the general ledger master file contains information about the type of account (balance sheet or profit & loss), the currency the account is maintained in, etc.

A *chart of accounts* is a collection of accounts. SAP delivers sample charts of accounts and it is common for companies to copy a sample chart and edit it to meet the specific business requirements of the company. In addition, during the course of business, it is often necessary to make changes or create new accounts in the chart of accounts.

In this section we will explore the creation of G/L accounts in the chart of accounts.

Among the transactions that are used to display and/or change the chart of accounts, we will explore the following:

- ▶ Display, create, or change an account in the chart of accounts (FSP0)
- ▶ Display, create, or change an account assigned to a company code (FSS0 or FS00)

To change an existing account, we navigate to the G/L account from the SAP Easy Access menu:

ACCOUNTING • FINANCIAL ACCOUNTING • GENERAL LEDGER • MASTER RECORDS • G/L ACCOUNTS • INDIVIDUAL PROCESSING • FSP0 – IN CHART OF ACCOUNTS

Transaction for account maintenance in a chart of accounts

 Rather than navigating to the transaction via the menu, you can type FSP0 in the command field and press Enter to access the screen for editing charts of accounts directly.

Let's display the data for account 474240 in chart of accounts INT1. We enter the account number in the G/L ACCOUNT field and the chart of accounts in the CHART OF ACCOUNTS field and then click 👓 to display the data.

Edit G/L Account Chart of accts data

Edit financial st [Display] ersion   Edit set   Edit cost element

| G/L Account | 474240 |
| Chart of Accts | INT1 |

👓 🖉 ▯ ▯   With Template   🔒 🗑

Edit

Type/Description | Key word/translation | Information

Control in chart of accounts

Account Group

◉ P&L statement acct

Detailed control for P&L statement accounts

Functional Area

○ Balance sheet account

Description

Short Text

G/L Acct Long Text

Consolidation data in chart of accounts

Figure 2.1: Displaying/editing a G/L account in a chart of accounts

Information about account 474240 in chart of accounts INT1 is now displayed. In Figure 2.2, we can see that the account is a profit and loss account for collecting other travel expenses. Had we chosen the editing icon 🖉, we would be able to make changes to attributes of the account.

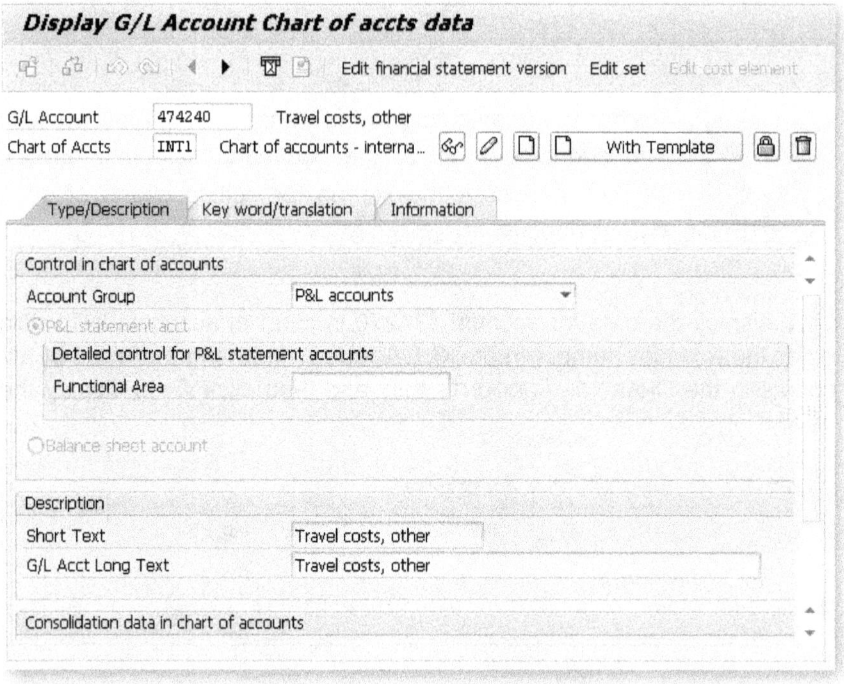

Display G/L Account Chart of accts data

Edit financial statement version   Edit set   Edit cost element

G/L Account   474240   Travel costs, other
Chart of Accts   INT1   Chart of accounts - interna...   With Template

| Type/Description | Key word/translation | Information |

Control in chart of accounts

Account Group   P&L accounts

◉ P&L statement acct

  Detailed control for P&L statement accounts

  Functional Area

○ Balance sheet account

Description

Short Text   Travel costs, other
G/L Acct Long Text   Travel costs, other

Consolidation data in chart of accounts

Figure 2.2: Displaying a G/L account in a chart of accounts

Let's create a new account, 474270 for travel expenses related to auto rentals, in chart of accounts INT1. We enter 474270 in the G/L ACCOUNT field, INT1 in the CHART OF ACCOUNTS FIELD, and then click ☐ With Template as shown in Figure 2.3. While we could have chosen ☐ to create the account, it is easier to copy the settings from an existing account (i.e., use a template) and then edit only the information that is different for our new account.

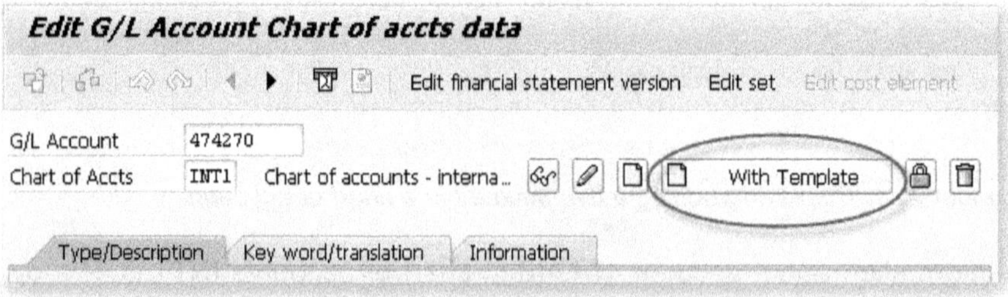

Edit G/L Account Chart of accts data

Edit financial statement version   Edit set   Edit cost element

G/L Account   474270
Chart of Accts   INT1   Chart of accounts - interna...   With Template

| Type/Description | Key word/translation | Information |

Figure 2.3: Creating a G/L account with a template

The SAP system now prompts you to enter the reference account (template) to be used for creating the account. Enter 474240 and chart of accounts INT1 and click ✔ to continue (Figure 2.4).

Figure 2.4: Entering the reference account

The text for the account to be created will need to be changed since it currently displays the text for account 474240 (Figure 2.5):

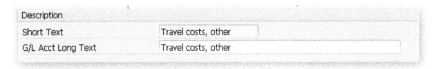

Figure 2.5: G/L account description

Change the text and then click 🖫 in the toolbar at the top of the screen to save the changes. Figure 2.6 shows the amended text.

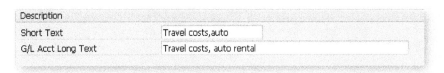

Figure 2.6: Changed G/L account description

A message confirms that the account has been saved (Figure 2.7):

Figure 2.7: Data saved message

If other languages are used in the chart of accounts, the system displays a reminder prompting you to check the names in the alternative languages (Figure 2.8). Save the record by clicking ✔.

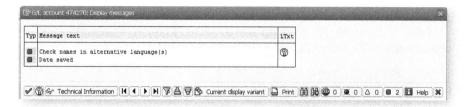

Figure 2.8: Messages displayed

If desired, from the account screen you can navigate to the KEY WORD/TRANSLATION tab and make changes to the text (Figure 2.9).

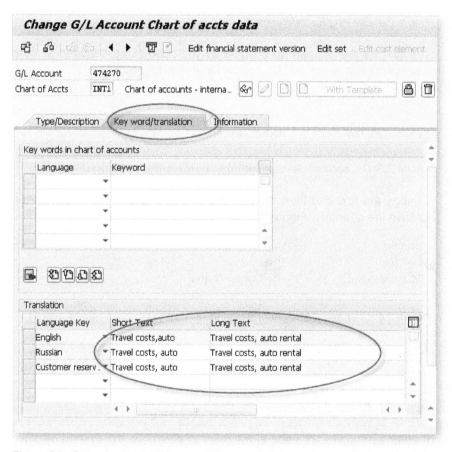

Figure 2.9: Changing the text for translation

Click 🖫 at the top of the screen and a message appears indicating that the changes have been saved.

Adding a G/L account to a company code

We have added a new account, 474270, to our chart of accounts INT1; however, it is not yet available in any company code. We can add individual accounts to a company code by accessing transaction FSS0 for editing G/L accounts in a company code.

To do so, we navigate to the G/L account from the SAP Easy Access menu:

ACCOUNTING • FINANCIAL ACCOUNTING • GENERAL LEDGER • MASTER RECORDS • G/L ACCOUNTS • INDIVIDUAL PROCESSING • FSS0 – IN COMPANY CODE

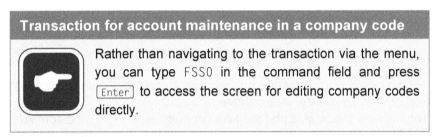

Transaction for account maintenance in a company code

Rather than navigating to the transaction via the menu, you can type FSS0 in the command field and press [Enter] to access the screen for editing company codes directly.

Enter the new G/L account 474270 and company code 5401 and then click ☐ to create the account in the company code (Figure 2.10).

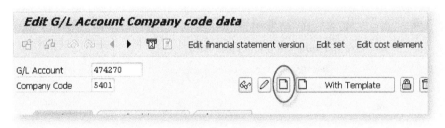

Figure 2.10: Creating an account in a company code

Note that the account number is displayed. Before we can create the account, we have to enter a field status group. Field status groups contain settings that determine which fields are required, optional, or suppressed when we post to the accounts. We will use the same field status group that was used for account 474240 in company code 5401. As shown in Figure 2.11, select the CREATE/BANK/INTEREST tab and enter G069 as the field status group. Save the entries by clicking 🖫.

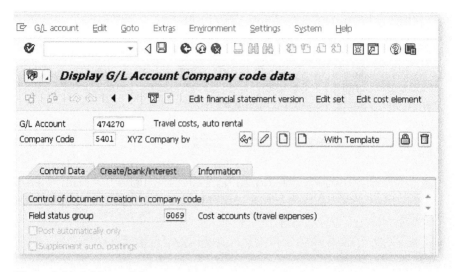

Figure 2.11: Adding a G/L account to a company code, field status group

We may also want to create our account in the other company codes. Rather than repeat the steps above, we can choose to perform this activity using a template. Enter the account number, 474270, and company code (in our example we are now creating the account in company code 5402) and click ▢ With Template (Figure 2.12).

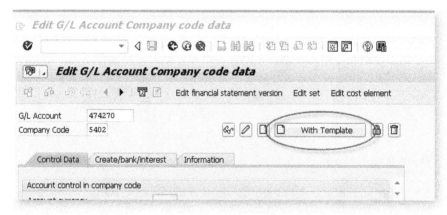

Figure 2.12: Adding a G/L account to a company code with a template

When prompted for the reference account to be used, enter account 474270 from company code 5401 and then click ✅ to continue (Figure 2.13).

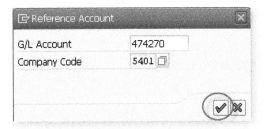

Figure 2.13: Entering the reference account

Note that the account information from company code 5401 has been copied to the record for company code 5402 (Figure 2.14). Click 🖫 to save the entries.

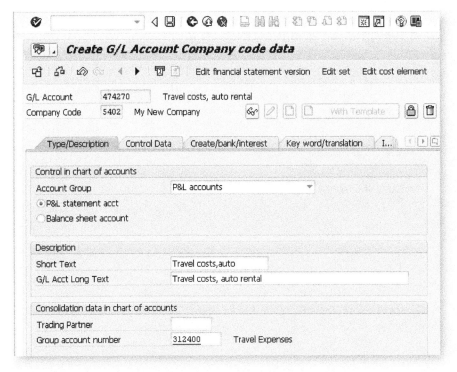

Figure 2.14: Creating a G/L account in another company code

Editing an existing G/L account

There will often be a need to make changes to an existing account. A common change is blocking an account for posting when the company decides that the account should no longer be used. Let's assume that the organization has decided that account 474290 should not be used in company 5402.

To block the account, we navigate to the G/L account from the SAP Easy Access menu:

ACCOUNTING • FINANCIAL ACCOUNTING • GENERAL LEDGER • MASTER RECORDS • G/L ACCOUNTS • INDIVIDUAL PROCESSING • FSS0 – IN COMPANY CODE

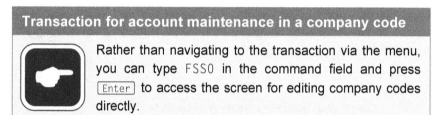

Transaction for account maintenance in a company code

Rather than navigating to the transaction via the menu, you can type FSS0 in the command field and press Enter to access the screen for editing company codes directly.

Enter the account and company code and then click 🔒 to block the account (Figure 2.15).

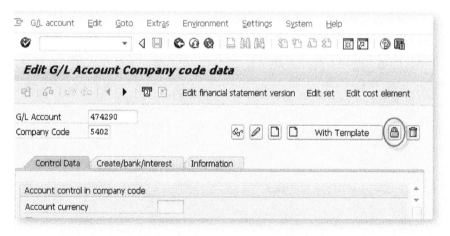

Figure 2.15: Editing an existing G/L account

Select the BLOCKED FOR POSTING indicator and click 💾 to save the entries (Figure 2.16).

We may also decide to flag the account for deletion by selecting 🗑 (Figure 2.17).

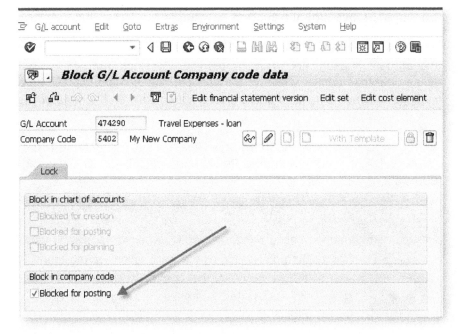

Figure 2.16: Blocking a G/L account for posting

Select the MARK FOR DELETION indicator and then click 🖫 to save the changes.

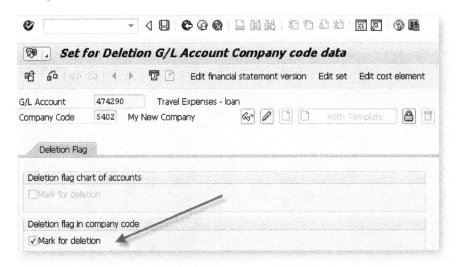

Figure 2.17: Flagging a G/L account for deletion

Editing a G/L account in a chart of accounts

There are many additional settings in a G/L account which control how the account is used. For example, there are settings that define what types of entries can be made to the account. We can access all of the settings by navigating to the G/L account from the SAP Easy Access menu:

ACCOUNTING • FINANCIAL ACCOUNTING • GENERAL LEDGER • MASTER RECORDS • G/L ACCOUNTS • INDIVIDUAL PROCESSING • FS00 – IN CHART OF ACCOUNTS

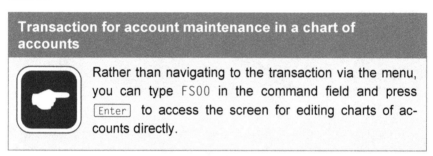

Transaction for account maintenance in a chart of accounts

Rather than navigating to the transaction via the menu, you can type FS00 in the command field and press Enter to access the screen for editing charts of accounts directly.

As we have seen when creating and editing accounts on the previous pages, the account maintenance screens contain many tabs. The fields displayed on these tabs depend on whether we are editing a balance sheet account or a profit and loss account. Figure 2.18 compares the control data for each type of account.

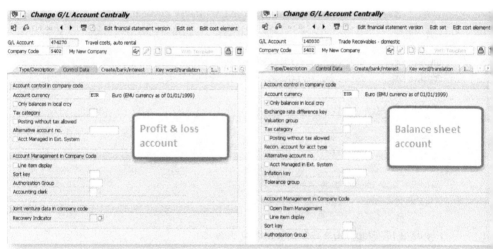

Figure 2.18: Profit & loss account; Balance sheet account

Many of the attributes on the account maintenance screens control functionality which is beyond the scope of this book; however, a brief discussion of some fields is included below.

▶ ACCOUNT GROUP

An account group is a means of classifying accounts. For example, balance sheet, P&L, fixed assets, materials management, etc.

▶ P&L STATEMENT ACCT BALANCE SHEET ACCT

All accounts have either the P&L or balance sheet account selected. This indicator controls the balance carried forward at year-end.

▶ SHORT TEXT/LONG TEXT

Texts are used for online display and reports. The space allowed on a particular screen or report determines which variant is used.

▶ ACCOUNT CURRENCY

It is possible for some accounts to have a different currency to the company code. For example, a US company might maintain a bank account in Canada and thus the account currency would be CAD. When a currency other than the company code currency is indicated, documents can only be posted in that currency. If the company code currency is used, documents can be posted in any currency.

▶ RECON. ACCOUNT FOR ACCT TYPE

Reconciliation accounts are used for integrating subledgers with the general ledger. Examples are vendor, customer, or asset accounts.

▶ OPEN ITEM MANAGEMENT

When this indicator is set, postings require one or more offsetting items to be posted to "clear" the open items. This is not the same as using reconciliation accounts — here there is no subledger. The setting is used for balance sheet accounts such as clearing accounts.

▶ LINE ITEM DISPLAY

This flag determines whether a user can display individual line items for the account. It should not be set for reconciliation accounts.

▶ FIELD STATUS GROUP

Field status groups can be defined to identify rules for document entry. The rules determine whether various fields are optional, mandatory, or suppressed when postings are entered.

▶ POST AUTOMATICALLY ONLY
If an account has this indicator selected, postings can only be entered by means of account determination (for example, from a valuation program) and you cannot enter a posting in the account using an online accounting entry.

2.2   What is SAP New GL?

Optional discussion: SAP New GL

The discussion of SAP New GL is not critical to learning about the G/L transactions presented in this book.

A general ledger (G/L) is the collection of master data and transaction data that is used by companies to measure financial performance and net worth. We now have G/L master data in our IDES environment to begin posting transactions. But before we do so, it might be helpful to have an explanation of *New GL*. Later on in the book you will notice that some menu paths include (NEW) in the description. This distinction is to separate these menu choices from Classic GL.

SAP Classic GL refers to releases of SAP GL software prior to SAP Enterprise Central Component (ECC) 5.0. SAP New GL was released by SAP in 2004 as part of SAP ECC 5.0. While the upgrade to ECC 5.0 from prior releases is not too challenging, migration to New GL is quite complex due to significant enhancements to functionality and table structures, and many SAP customers have chosen not to switch to New GL. SAP continues to support *Classic GL;* but any new customers must implement New GL.

The examples in this book have all been created in a New GL environment. Since a detailed discussion of New GL could fill an entire book, let's just take a brief look at some of the features.

2.2.1   Parallel accounting

Often, large organizations are faced with the challenge of following more than one set of accounting rules due, for example, to legal requirements. Large organizations may have entities in different countries, each with different reporting requirements. Another example is that the insurance industry has to follow different rules for reporting to the Securities and Exchange Commission (SEC) than it does for reporting to state regulatory bodies.

One method of managing diverse reporting requirements would be to establish separate, parallel G/L accounts for recording adjustments to accommodate the different accounting standards. Reports could then be created based only on the accounts appropriate for the particular requirement for any given situation. Depreciation of assets provides another example of where accounting rules vary. Depreciation allowed according to tax regulations generally varies from depreciation that is reported in a company's financial reports. Companies could set up separate depreciation accounts to record the difference in valuation or even maintain spreadsheets outside of the accounting system to reconcile the differences in the valuation of assets. In a large organization with many accounts, managing reporting requirements with parallel accounts or external spreadsheets can be quite challenging.

With SAP New GL, separate ledgers are used for the different accounting standards and parallel accounts. The SAP system will contain a leading ledger and one or more parallel ledgers which are used for different valuations. Accounting documents where there is no difference in valuation are posted to all ledgers simultaneously by the SAP software. You can choose, however, to post entries only to a parallel ledger. Reporting can then be filtered by ledger in order to meet various reporting requirements and the number of accounts does not need to be extended.

2.2.2   Segment reporting

Large companies are required to report financial results by operating segment. An operating segment may be defined as a part of the business that has a common production process, a common type of product or service, a common group of customers, or is required by a regulatory agency to have unique reporting. As an example, a large integrated paper-based packaging company might report earnings in three segments:

recycling, corrugated packaging, and consumer packaging. A large oil and gas company might report segments of upstream, downstream, chemicals and financing.

In Classic GL, the organizational characteristic **Business Area** was available to facilitate segment reporting in an SAP system. However, many SAP customers chose to use the business area for different purposes. With New GL, an additional characteristic, **Segment,** was introduced specifically for segment reporting.

2.2.3   Document splitting

The accounting *closing process* involves closing out all profit and loss accounts to equity. You may recall the *accounting formula* from Chapter 1:

Assets – liabilities = owner's equity

With simple algebra, we can change this formula to:

Assets – liabilities – owner's equity = 0

With Classic GL, a net zero balance sheet was only available by company code or business area. New GL enables companies to choose other levels such as profit center or segment for a net zero balance sheet.

Let's assume that we have an invoice from a vendor which is for services provided to two profit centers. The accounting entry is a credit to a vendor account payable and two debits, one to each of the two profit centers. The functionality of document splitting causes the credit side of the entry to be "split" behind the scenes to the two separate profit centers. Furthermore, when payment is made to the vendor, although the accounting entry is a simple credit to cash and a debit to the vendor account payable, once again the SAP system splits the cash entry over the same profit centers as were reflected when the original vendor invoice was recorded.

In New GL, there are two views of accounting entries: a document entry view and an accounting view. The accounting view reflects document splitting. Document splitting enables net zero balance sheet reporting at the level defined by the business.

2.2.4   Integration of CO and FI

In previous sections we have mentioned CO or the Controlling module in SAP. In contrast with the FI module, which is used for external financial reporting, the Controlling module is used for internal or management reporting.

An example of a function of the Controlling module is the allocation of overhead expenses to various cost centers. The Controlling module includes the functionality for (temporarily) accumulating costs in other cost objects besides the cost center, such as a project or internal order. These costs can then be transferred or settled to an asset or to a destination cost center.

With Classic GL, a separate reconciliation ledger was maintained in SAP for reconciling CO to FI. With New GL, there is automatic, real-time integration of CO and FI, rendering the reconciliation ledger and process obsolete.

2.2.5   Extensible totals tables

To facilitate reporting, the SAP system summarizes transactions in totals tables. With Classic GL, the totals table (GLT0) contained a limited number of characteristics for reporting. In order to enhance reporting, a Special Purpose Ledger application was provided by SAP. This application required significant configuration and periodic processes in order to remain synchronized with FI.

With New GL, the totals table (FAGLFLEXT) not only contains more characteristics, but customer-specific fields can also be included in the table. While Special Purpose Ledger is still available, it may not be needed by many organizations.

2.2.6 Classic vs New GL

Table 2.1 provides a comparison of Classic and New GL.

Functionality	Classic GL	New GL
Parallel accounting	Parallel accounts used for valuation differences	Parallel ledgers available for valuation differences
Segment reporting	Business area used for segment reporting	Segment field introduced specifically for segment reporting
Document splitting	Zero balance sheet available only at company code and business area level	Zero balance sheet available at user-defined levels
FI-CO integration	Reconciliation ledger maintained and month-end process required for reconciling FI and CO	FI and CO real-time integration
Totals table for reporting	GLT0 Limited reporting characteristics Special Purpose Ledgers required for any enhanced reporting	FAGLFLEXT Additional characteristics included User-defined characteristics can be included

Table 2.1: Classic vs New GL

2.3 G/L transactions

With our understanding of accounting and the basic master data in the SAP system, we are now ready to learn how to post transactions in the SAP system!

As we will see in the following sections, SAP provides many different options for posting general ledger transactions. We will cover the most common transactions.

2.3.1   F-02/FB01L: Entering a G/L account document

You may wonder why there are two transaction codes listed for entering a simple G/L account document. New GL was discussed in Section 2.2. F-02 is the Classic GL posting document transaction and FB01L is the New GL transaction. F-02 can also be used in New GL; the difference between the two transactions is that FB01L enables the user to enter a ledger or a ledger group. Figure 2.19 illustrates the difference between the two transactions.

Figure 2.19: Comparison of F-02 and FB01L

With New GL, we can post to one ledger or a group of ledgers. If no ledger is specified in a G/L transaction, the transaction is posted to all ledgers.

Let's use transaction FB01L to post a G/L account document in the SAP system in order to make the following adjustment:

DR.   Company Car Costs $1000
CR.   Accounts Payable – Affiliates $1000

From the SAP Easy Access menu, navigate to:

ACCOUNTING • FINANCIAL ACCOUNTING • GENERAL LEDGER • DOCUMENT ENTRY • FB01L – ENTER GENERAL POSTING FOR LEDGER GROUP

Entering general postings for a ledger group

Rather than navigating via the menu, you can type FB01L in the command field and press [Enter] to access the GENERAL POSTING FOR LEDGER GROUP screen directly.

On the FB01L entry screen, we enter header data first (Figure 2.20):

General Posting for Ledger Group: Header Data

Held Document   Account Model   ☒Fast Data Entry   ⬚Post with reference   ✎ Editing Options

Document Date	11/2/2014	[1]	Type	SA [2]	Company Code	5401 [3]
Posting Date	11/30/2014	[4]	Period	11 [5]	Currency/Rate	EUR [6] [7]
Document Number		[8]	Ledger Grp	OL	[9] Translatn Date	[10]
Reference	ADJ-01	[11]			Cross-CC no.	[12]
Doc.Header Text	Adjust car costs	[13]				
Trading part.BA	[14]					

Figure 2.20: Entering header data for a G/L posting

❶ DOCUMENT DATE: represents the date of an original document, for example the date on an invoice received from a vendor.

❷ TYPE: document types are configured in the SAP system and control the posting rules to be applied. The configuration of document types is beyond the scope of this book. Note that each document type in the SAP system is assigned a number range which is applied when the document is posted.

❸ COMPANY CODE: represents the company code where the document is posted.

❹ POSTING DATE: the date the transaction was recorded in the accounting system; it can be different to the document date. In our example, we are using the last day of the accounting period as the posting date. Note that the SAP system also records an entry date which is the system date on the day the entry was actually created in the SAP system.

❺ PERIOD: represents the accounting period in which the transaction is recorded. The configuration of posting periods is beyond the scope of this book; however, note that the posting date must fall within the posting period definitions.

Posting periods

 Posting periods are defined in *fiscal year variants*. SAP delivers several fiscal year variants, the most common of which is K4, specifying a calendar year of 12 posting periods that match calendar months and 4 special periods that can be used for adjustments. You can use transaction 0B29 to view fiscal year variants and the posting periods.

Transaction 0B52 is used to open or close posting periods for activity.

⑥ CURRENCY: represents the currency in which the transaction is recorded. The currency can be different to the currency configured for the company code, in which case the SAP system applies configured currency rates to the transaction. SAP transaction records can reflect at least three currencies: transaction currency (the document currency), local currency (company code currency), and group currency (reporting currency).

⑦ RATE: can be input to override the currency rate tables that are normally applied to transactions. This field is optional; if no rate is entered, the rate tables in the SAP system are used. Exchange rates are usually entered via an upload from a service. The details for managing currency rates are beyond the scope of this book.

⑧ DOCUMENT NUMBER: generally assigned by the SAP system using a configured number range for each document type; however, you can also enter document numbers manually. The use of SAP-assigned document numbers is recommended.

⑨ LEDGER GROUP: can be entered in order to specify the ledger or group of ledgers in which the transaction should be posted. The configuration of ledgers and ledger groups, features of SAP New GL, are beyond the scope of this book. If no ledger group is entered, then the transaction is posted to all of the ledgers assigned to the company code. In our example, we are specifying 0L, which is the leading ledger, and the transaction is thus posted only to the leading ledger.

⑩ TRANSLATION DATE: used for translating a transaction that is recorded in a currency other than the company code currency. This is an optional field; if no date is entered, the translation uses the rate in effect as of the document entry date.

⑪ REFERENCE: a user-defined reference that can later be used for searching for documents to display or edit.

⑫ CROSS-CC NO.: generally assigned by SAP company codes for documents which contain line items in two different company codes. A concatenation of the configured number range for each document type and the company code involved is used. Similar to the document number, you can enter document numbers manually; however, the use of SAP-assigned cross-company code document numbers is recommended.

⑬ DOCUMENT HEADER TEXT: a short explanation pertaining to the entire accounting document.

⑭ TRADING PART. BA: a field that is used by the SAP system with inter-company eliminations.

After completing the header information, begin data entry (Figure 2.21) for the first detail line in the document and then click the Enter icon ✅ in the upper left corner of the toolbar to save the entries.

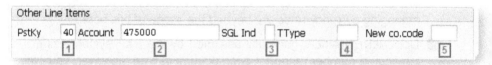

Figure 2.21: Entering line item data for the first detail line

❶ PSTKY: an abbreviation for *posting key*. Posting keys determine how the entry is posted. There are posting keys for G/L account transactions, customer account transactions, asset account transactions, etc. In addition to determining whether the entry is a debit or a credit, the posting key is also the basis for the application of other posting rules. Posting keys can be configured; however, most are delivered by SAP. The most common posting keys delivered which we will encounter in this book are listed in Table 2.2.

Posting Key	Description
40	GL account debit posting
50	GL account credit posting
01	Customer invoice (debit)
11	Customer credit (credit)
25	Vendor payment (debit)
31	Vendor invoice (credit)

Table 2.2: Posting keys

❷ ACCOUNT: the general ledger account for the first line item.

Using SAP dropdowns

 To the right of many fields you will find a dropdown icon 🗗 which enables you to search for input values.

❸ SGL IND: an abbreviation for *Special G/L Indicator*. This field is used for specific types of transactions, for example down payments, generally with vendor or customer transactions. In our example we will leave the SGL IND field blank as we are posting a simple general ledger entry.

❹ TTYPE: an abbreviation for *transaction type*. Transaction types are used with fixed asset transactions. In our example we will leave the TTYPE field blank as we are not posting a fixed asset transaction.

❺ NEW CO. CODE: does not appear with the first line item. It appears for subsequent line items to enable transactions which impact more than one company code.

After clicking the ENTER icon 🗹 enter additional information pertaining to the line item. Most notable in our example is the line item amount and the text. If required by the configuration for the company code, you can enter other information, such as the cost center. Selecting the additional assignment icon ⇨ allows you to enter further data.

In our example (Figure 2.22), we enter only an amount and a text to describe the line item. In addition, we begin the input for the second line item by entering the posting key and account.

Enter G/L Account Document: Add G/L account item

⚮ 🖫 🖻 🗇 ➦ More data   Account Model   🖳 Fast Data Entry

| G/L Account | 475000 | Company car costs |
| Company Code | 5401 XYZ Company bv | |

Item 1 / Debit entry / 40

Amount	1000	EUR
Cost Center		Order	
WBS Element		Profit. Segment	⇨
Network		Real Estate Obj	⇨
Functional Area		Sales Order	
			⇨ More
		Quantity	
		Due On	
Assignment			
Text	Adjusting Car Costs for Johannes Bremer		🖉 Long Texts

Next Line Item

| PstKy | 50 | Account | 165099 | SGL Ind | | TType | | New co.code | |

Figure 2.22: Details for the first line item

Just as with the first line item of our general ledger document, we can enter additional details pertaining to the second line item (Figure 2.23). Because we are creating an entry for a specific balance sheet account, we are also presented with the VALUE DATE field. This date is used in currency valuation calculations, if there are any, when posting a document in a currency other than the company code currency. The SAP system enters the document entry date as the default.

Enter G/L account document: Add G/L account item

👤 📋 📋 🗐 ☞More data   Account Model ☑Fast Data Entry

G/L Account   165099   Accounts Payable - Affiliates, adjustment acct.
Company Code   5401 XYZ Company bv

Item 2 / Credit entry / 50		
Amount	1000	EUR
Business Area		Trdg part.BA
Cost Center		
Profit Center		
Functional Area		⇨ More
Value date	11/02/2014	
Assignment		Asst retirement ☐
Text	Johannes Bremer car cost change	✐ Long Texts

Figure 2.23: Details for the second line item

Since we are not entering any additional line items, we are ready to post the entry. We may want to validate our entries before attempting to post and we can do this by selecting DOCUMENT • SIMULATE from the toolbar (Figure 2.24):

Figure 2.24: Simulating in order to check the document before posting

The document to be posted is displayed (Figure 2.25). If there were any errors, messages would appear at the bottom of the screen.

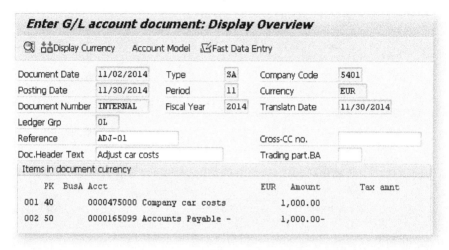

Figure 2.25: Document ready to be posted

Note that the toolbar, as shown in Figure 2.26, contains options for further display or editing prior to posting.

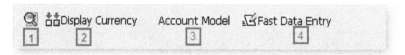

Figure 2.26: Document display/edit options

❶ Allows you to go back to the details of a particular line item for editing.

❷ Changes the display currency (useful if the document currency is different to the company code currency).

❸ Account models are pre-determined line items which can be created in order to streamline data entry.

❹ Clicking FAST DATA ENTRY displays a screen for adding line items to the entry faster than one at a time (Figure 2.27):

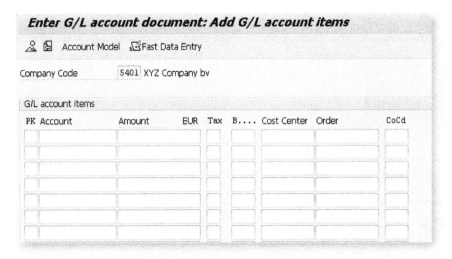

Figure 2.27: Fast data entry for adding line items to a G/L account document

Since we have no errors to correct and we are only posting a two-line entry, we can click 🖫 in the middle of the toolbar at the top of the screen to post our entry. The SAP system returns a confirmation message (Figure 2.28) that includes the document number assigned:

Figure 2.28: Document posted and document number assigned

2.3.2 FB50/FB50L: Entering a G/L account document

Transactions FB50 (Classic GL) and FB50L (New GL) are similar to F-02 and FB01L, and in fact execute the same posting program. You may develop you own transaction preference for posting general ledger documents depending on business needs. Let's take a look at posting with FB50L.

From the SAP Easy Access menu, navigate to:

ACCOUNTING • FINANCIAL ACCOUNTING • GENERAL LEDGER • DOCUMENT ENTRY • FB50 – ENTER G/L ACCOUNT DOCUMENT FOR LEDGER GROUP

Entering G/L account documents for a ledger group

 Rather than navigating via the menu, you can type FB50L in the command field and press [Enter] to access the G/L ACCOUNT DOCUMENT FOR LEDGER GROUP screen directly.

The differences between the first screen that appears with F-02/FB01L and FB50/FB50L are identified below (Figure 2.29):

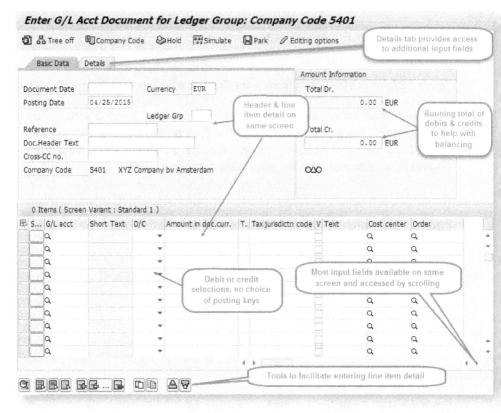

Figure 2.29: FB50/FB50L entry screen

On the screen illustrated in Figure 2.30, we have entered data to post another adjustment to our company car costs. Note that the entry balances and therefore it can be posted, as evidenced by the green indicator under the amount information fields at the top right of the screen.

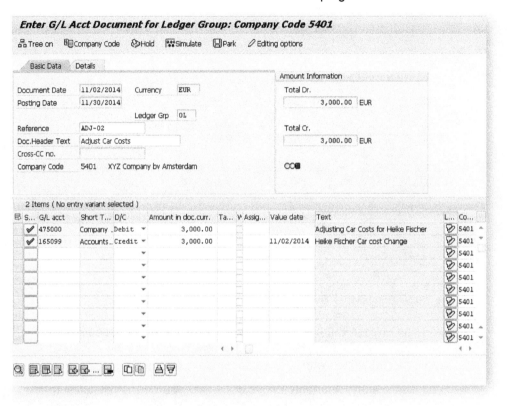

Figure 2.30: G/L account document details entered

Before we post the document, let's explore some of the tools for editing and posting (Figure 2.31).

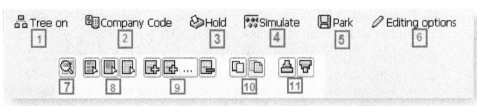

Figure 2.31: FB50/FB50L editing tools

47

1 The TREE ON option displays or hides a navigation pane to the left of the entry screen which allows you to access screen variants (screen layouts configured for specific entry requirements), access account assignment templates, or select previously entered documents that were placed on hold (see Figure 2.32).

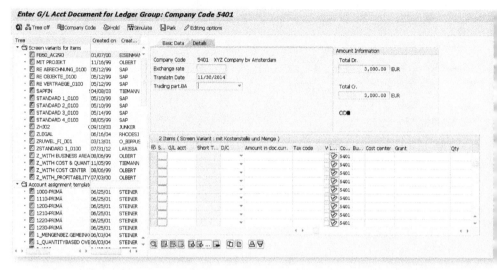

Figure 2.32: FB50/FB50L, Tree on

2 You can change the company code for an entry at the header level. Line items would then default to the specified company code but could be overwritten with a different company code.

3 You can place documents on hold so that you can come back to them at a future point in time to edit and/or process them to completion.

4 The SIMULATE option simulates the posting as we saw with F-02/FB01L.

5 Documents that are complete can be parked; they are not posted, but can be retrieved at a future date for posting.

6 Clicking EDITING OPTIONS displays the screen shown in Figure 2.33, enabling you to select options for editing G/L account documents. After selecting any options required, click 🖫 in the toolbar at the top of the screen to save and return to the entry screen. These options are retained for your user ID for subsequent entries until you change them again.

Accounting Editing Options

Document entry

General Entry Options	Default document currency
☐ Documents only in local currency	⦿ Local currency
☐ Amount fields only for document currency	○ Last document currency used
☐ Exchange rate from first line item	○ None
☐ No special G/L transactions	
☐ Documents not cross-company code	**Default Company Code**
☐ Documents must be complete for parking	☐ No Company Code Proposal
☐ No partner business area in head.screen	
☐ Calculate taxes on net amount	
☐ Copy text for G/L account entry	
☐ Do not copy tax code	
☐ Fast entry via ISR number	
☐ ISR Entry with Control Display	
☐ Do not update control totals	
☐ Automatic Negative Posting	

Special options for single screen transactions

☐ Hide transaction	Doc.type option ⬚ Document type hidden ▾
☐ Propose final amount	☐ Document date equals pstg date
☐ D/C indicator as +/- sign	☐ Complex Search for Business Partner
☐ Display periods	☐ Propose Last Tax Code
☐ Posting in special periods possible	☐ Tax Code: Only Display Short Text
☐ Always Use Payment Base Deadline	

Figure 2.33: Accounting editing options

❼ You can choose the detail icon 🔍 after selecting a line in the G/L account document. A detail entry screen as shown in Figure 2.23 appears for input.

❽ The line selection icons 🔲🔲🔲 enable you to select all lines, select a block of lines, or deselect a previous selection for subsequent processing such as deletion or editing.

❾ Use the icons 🔲, 🔲 ..., or 🔲 to add one row, several rows, or delete rows.

❿ Copy icons 🔲🔲 allow you to copy lines or fields to a new line.

⓫ You can choose sorting icons 🔲🔲 after selecting a column header to sort the lines in the G/L account document.

To post the entry, click 🖫 in the toolbar at the top of the screen. The SAP system returns a message noting that the document has been posted (Figure 2.34):

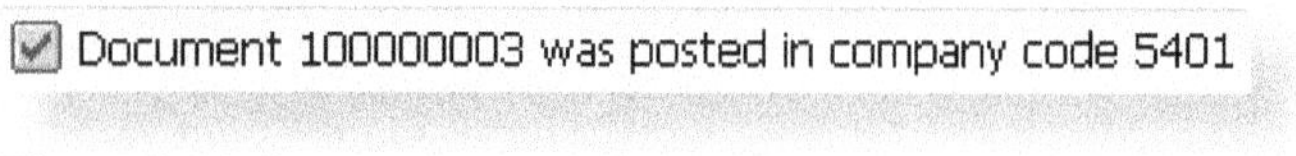

✓ Document 100000003 was posted in company code 5401

Figure 2.34: Document posted message

2.3.3   FV50/FV50L: Parked documents

Users can enter documents and, instead of posting them, park them for posting at a later point in time. This functionality is useful if a user does not have authorization for posting but is responsible for creating an entry. The first user parks the document and a second user posts the document.

To access the document parking functionality, from the SAP Easy Access menu, navigate to:

ACCOUNTING • FINANCIAL ACCOUNTING • GENERAL LEDGER • DOCUMENT ENTRY • FV50L – PARK G/L ACCOUNT DOCUMENT FOR LEDGER GROUP

Parking G/L account documents
Rather than navigating via the menu, you can type FV50L in the command field and press ⌈Enter⌉ to access the PARK G/L ACCOUNT DOCUMENT screen directly.

The entry screen is almost the same as FB50/FB50L; however an additional icon, 🖫 Save as completed, allows the user to park the document (Figure 2.35):

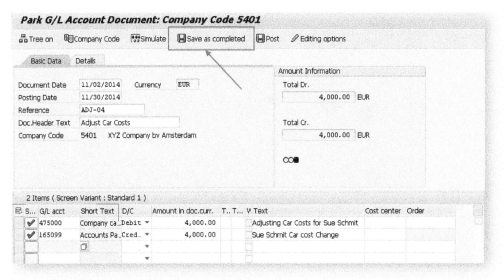

Figure 2.35: Parking a document

Once this option is selected, the SAP system returns a message (Figure 2.36) which includes a document number for the parked document. There is no impact to the general ledger for this document.

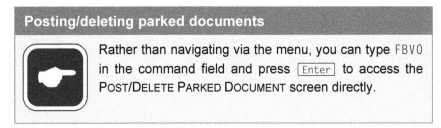

Figure 2.36: Parked document

To post the parked document, from the SAP Easy Access menu, navigate to: ACCOUNTING • FINANCIAL ACCOUNTING • GENERAL LEDGER • DOCUMENT • PARKED DOCUMENTS • FBV0 – POST/DELETE

Posting/deleting parked documents

Rather than navigating via the menu, you can type FBV0 in the command field and press [Enter] to access the POST/DELETE PARKED DOCUMENT screen directly.

On the initial screen (Figure 2.37), enter the company code and choose DOCUMENT LIST from the menu bar.

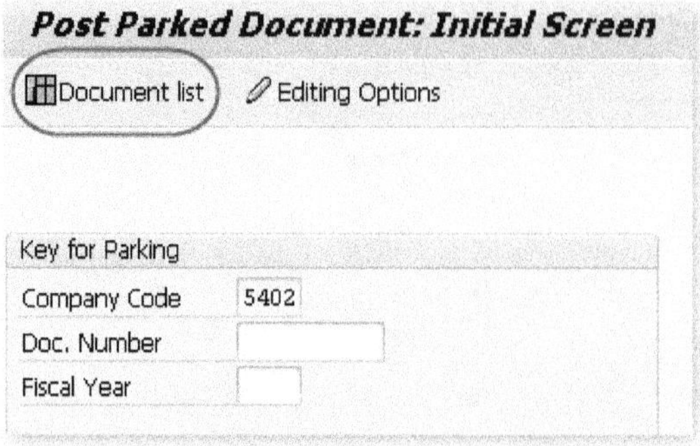

Post Parked Document: Initial Screen

(⊞ Document list)   ∥ Editing Options

Key for Parking

Company Code	5402
Doc. Number	
Fiscal Year	

Figure 2.37: Initial screen for posting parked documents

On the LIST OF PARKED DOCUMENTS screen (Figure 2.38), you can enter criteria to filter the list that will be presented. In our example we will select parked documents by the user who entered the documents. Click ⊕ to execute and continue.

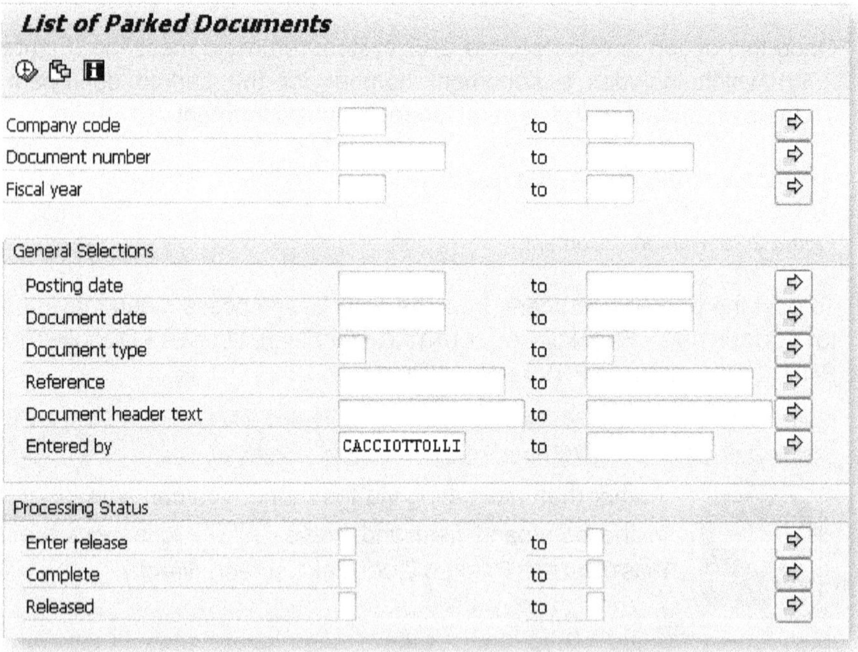

List of Parked Documents

⊕ ⅏ ⯐

Company code		to	⇨
Document number		to	⇨
Fiscal year		to	⇨

General Selections

Posting date		to	⇨
Document date		to	⇨
Document type		to	⇨
Reference		to	⇨
Document header text		to	⇨
Entered by	CACCIOTTOLLI	to	⇨

Processing Status

Enter release		to	⇨
Complete		to	⇨
Released		to	⇨

Figure 2.38: Filter criteria selection for the list of parked documents

In the list that is returned (Figure 2.39), double-click the parked document that you wish to post.

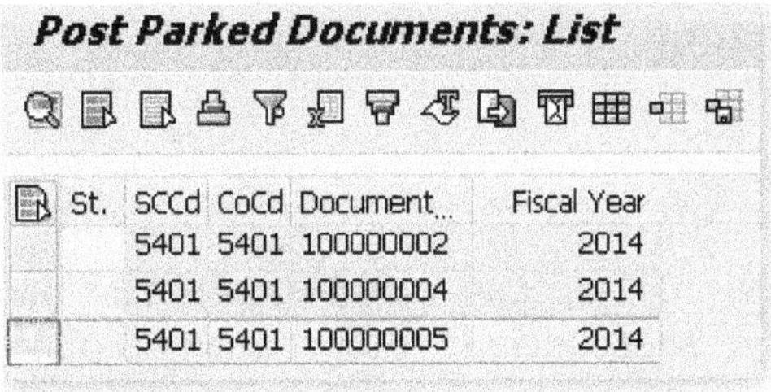

Figure 2.39: List of parked documents

The selected document is now available for editing or posting. Click the relevant icon for posting, as shown in Figure 2.40.

Figure 2.40: Posting a parked document

The SAP system returns a message stating that the document has been posted (Figure 2.41).

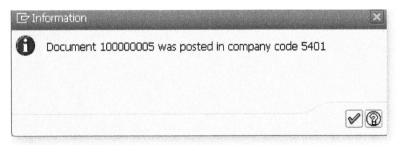

Figure 2.41: Parked document has been posted

2.3.4   F-04: Posting with clearing

What is posting with clearing?

You may recall from Section 2.1.1 G/L accounts, that certain accounts are set up to manage open items. These include reconciliation accounts (customer or vendor accounts) and accounts managed on an open item basis. Posting with clearing applies to transactions that have been recorded in such accounts.

Posting with clearing results in a clearing document which is noted in the transactions which are chosen when the posting with clearing transaction is completed.

Posting an open item

In order to demonstrate posting with clearing, we first need to post a transaction to an account managed on an open item basis. Posting to customer and vendor reconciliation accounts will be discussed in Chapters 3 and 4.

We will use transaction code FB50 as demonstrated in Section 2.3.2. We will post a debit to account 159100 (Other Receivables) and a credit to an expense account 417000 (Purchased Services). Remember to press the ⌨Enter⌨ key to bypass any warning messages that may appear.

The FB50 entry screen for our document 100000000 is shown in Figure 2.42.

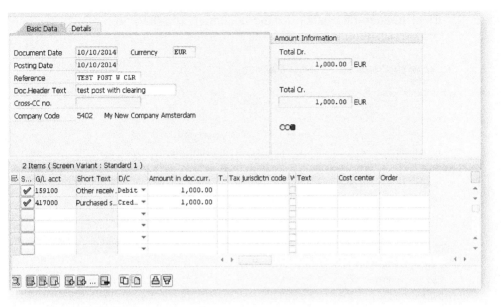

Figure 2.42: Posting an open item

Posting with clearing

We are now ready to create a post with clearing document. We will clear the open item document 100000000 that we created previously.

1. From the SAP Easy Access menu, navigate to: ACCOUNTING • FINANCIAL ACCOUNTING • GENERAL LEDGER • DOCUMENT ENTRY • F-04 – POST WITH CLEARING.

Posting with clearing

Rather than navigating to the POST WITH CLEARING screen via the menu, you can type F-04 in the command field and press Enter to access the screen directly.

---

2. Enter header information for the document and then select CHOOSE OPEN ITEMS (Figure 2.43).

Figure 2.43: Posting with clearing, step 2

3. In our example, we know the document number that we wish to clear, so we choose the document number option from the additional selections on the right (Figure 2.44). However, we could choose items based upon other criteria. After making your selection(s), choose PROCESS OPEN ITEMS.

4. Enter the document number that we wish to clear and then select PROCESS OPEN ITEMS (Figure 2.45).

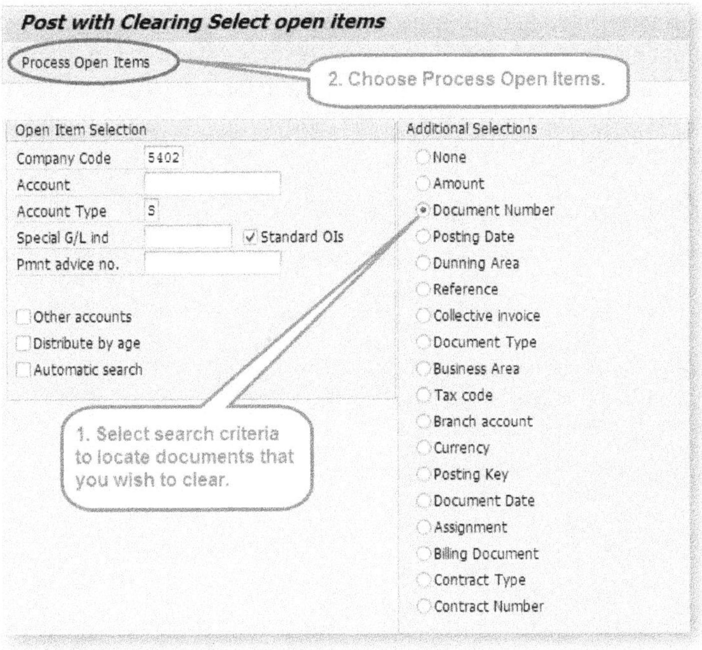

Post with Clearing Select open items

Process Open Items

2. Choose Process Open Items.

Open Item Selection		Additional Selections
Company Code	5402	○ None
Account		○ Amount
Account Type	S	⦿ Document Number
Special G/L ind	☑ Standard OIs	○ Posting Date
Pmnt advice no.		○ Dunning Area
		○ Reference
☐ Other accounts		○ Collective invoice
☐ Distribute by age		○ Document Type
☐ Automatic search		○ Business Area
		○ Tax code
		○ Branch account
		○ Currency
		○ Posting Key
		○ Document Date
		○ Assignment
		○ Billing Document
		○ Contract Type
		○ Contract Number

1. Select search criteria to locate documents that you wish to clear.

Figure 2.44: Posting with clearing, step 3

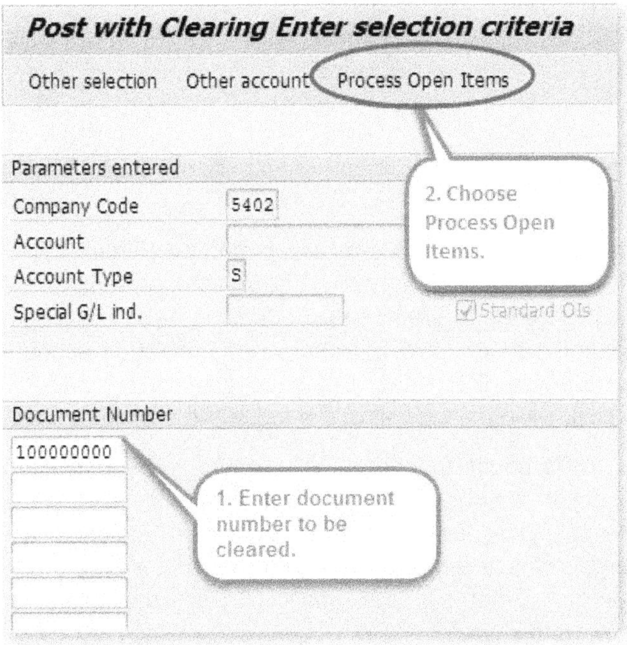

Post with Clearing Enter selection criteria

Other selection   Other account   Process Open Items

Parameters entered

Company Code	5402
Account	
Account Type	S
Special G/L ind.	☑ Standard OIs

2. Choose Process Open Items.

Document Number

100000000

1. Enter document number to be cleared.

Figure 2.45: Posting with clearing, step 4

5. In our example (Figure 2.46), only one open item is listed; however, in a production environment, depending on the selections in step 3, additional line items may be activated or deactivated. The total number of items and total value assigned shown at the bottom of the screen will change accordingly.

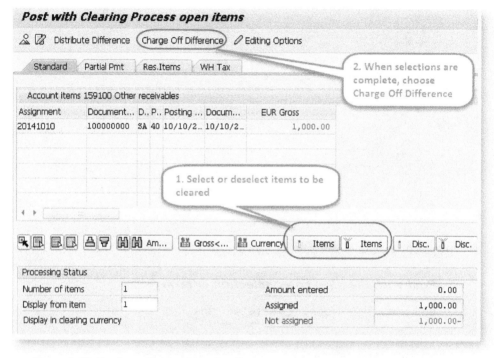

Figure 2.46: Posting with clearing, step 5

6. Next we choose the offset for the items being cleared (Figure 2.47). Since we are clearing a debit item, we will be posting a credit to the customer account. Therefore, we need an offsetting debit to charge. Debits have posting key 40. We will charge the offset to account 449900 – Other General Expenses. Enter the posting key and account and then click 💾 in the toolbar at the top of the screen to save.

7. Next we enter the amount to charge to account 449000 (Figure 2.48). In our example, we charge the entire amount. However, if the amount is to be split between different accounts, an additional account to be charged can be entered in the NEXT LINE ITEM area at the bottom of the screen. Enter 1000.00 and click 💾 in the toolbar at the top of the screen to save.

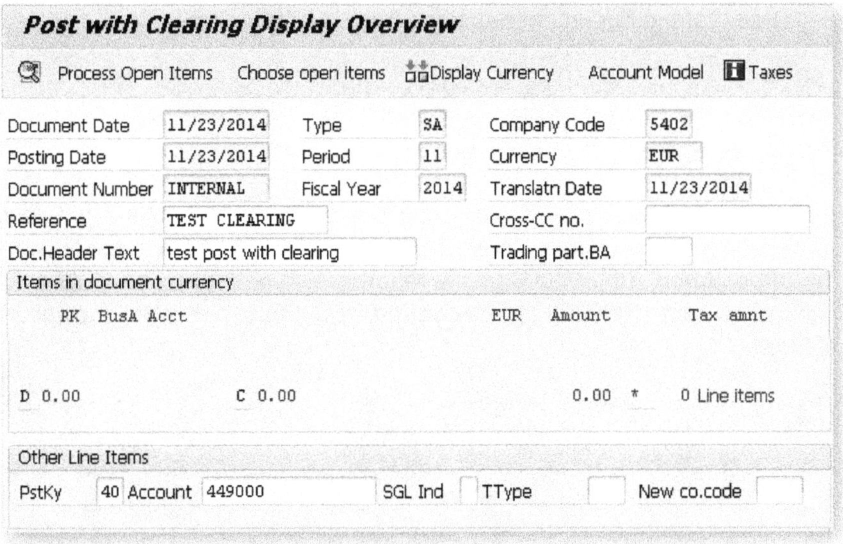

Post with Clearing Display Overview

Process Open Items   Choose open items   Display Currency   Account Model   Taxes

Document Date	11/23/2014	Type	SA
Posting Date	11/23/2014	Period	11
Document Number	INTERNAL	Fiscal Year	2014
Reference	TEST CLEARING		
Doc.Header Text	test post with clearing		

Company Code 5402
Currency EUR
Translatn Date 11/23/2014
Cross-CC no.
Trading part.BA

Items in document currency

PK BusA Acct   EUR Amount   Tax amnt

D 0.00   C 0.00   0.00 *   0 Line items

Other Line Items

PstKy 40 Account 449000   SGL Ind TType   New co.code

Figure 2.47: Posting with clearing, step 6

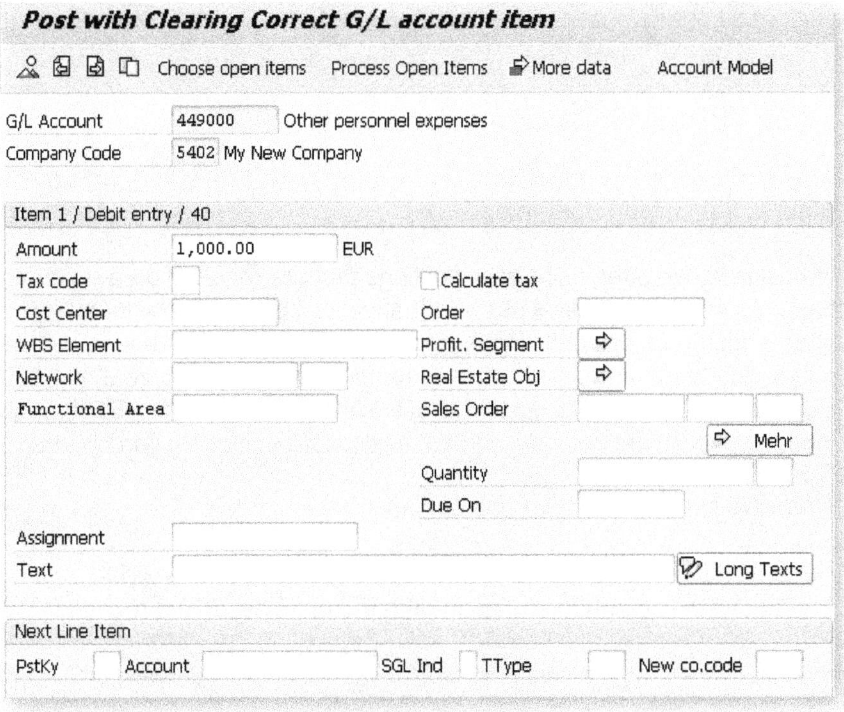

Post with Clearing Correct G/L account item

Choose open items   Process Open Items   More data   Account Model

G/L Account 449000   Other personnel expenses
Company Code 5402 My New Company

Item 1 / Debit entry / 40

Amount	1,000.00	EUR
Tax code		Calculate tax
Cost Center		Order
WBS Element		Profit. Segment
Network		Real Estate Obj
Functional Area		Sales Order
		Mehr
		Quantity
		Due On
Assignment		
Text		Long Texts

Next Line Item

PstKy Account   SGL Ind TType   New co.code

Figure 2.48: Posting with clearing, step 7

8. Note that the document has been posted (Figure 2.49).

☑ Document 100000001 was posted in company code 5402

Figure 2.49: Posting with clearing, step 8

In Section 2.3.8 we will review listing posted documents. As a preview, from the screen shown in Figure 2.50, we can see that our original posting of document 100000000 to the receivable account has been cleared with document 100000001. Document 100000001 is also shown as cleared.

G/L Account	159100	Other receivables
Company Code	5402	
Ledger	0L	

	St	DocumentNo	Typ	Doc. Date	PK	Amount in local cur.	LCurr	Clrng doc.	Text
	▣	100000000	SA	10/10/2014	40	1,000.00	EUR	100000001	
	▣	100000001	SA	11/23/2014	50	1,000.00-	EUR	100000001	let's clear document 100000000
*	▣					0.00	EUR		
** Account 159100						0.00	EUR		

Figure 2.50: Posting with clearing, document display

2.3.5   FBD1/F-14: Recurring documents

What is a recurring document?

In business, we often encounter postings that are required on a recurring basis. As an example, let's assume that you will be paid an annual bonus after working so diligently during the year. Although the bonus will be paid in the last month, the business requires a monthly accrual of 1,000 to be made. It is not necessary to use transaction FB50 or FB50L each month to record the accrual; instead, a recurring document can be used.

There are two steps to recurring documents:

1. A recurring document is created (once)

2. A posting is created referencing the recurring document (periodic)

Creating recurring documents

Let's first create the document to accrue the annual bonus.

1. From the SAP Easy Access menu navigate to: ACCOUNTING • FINAN-
   CIAL ACCOUNTING • GENERAL LEDGER • DOCUMENT ENTRY • REFERENCE
   DOCUMENTS • FBD1 – RECURRING DOCUMENT.

Creating recurring documents

 Rather than navigating to the recurring document transaction via the menu, you can type FBD1 in the command
field and press [Enter] to access the recurring entry
creation screen directly.

---

2. Enter information pertaining to the recurrence (Figure 2.51), the document header, and the first line item and press [Enter] once you
   have finished. The debit (posting key 40) for expense account
   433000 will be entered first in our example.

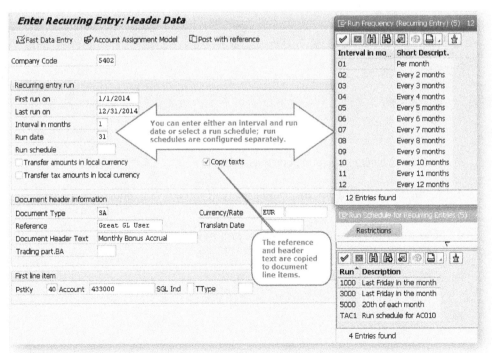

Figure 2.51: Creating a recurring document, step 2

3. Enter the amount for the debit (posting key 40). In the NEXT LINE ITEM section, enter posting key 50 (credit) and the accrual account 204000 and click 💾 to save (Figure 2.52).

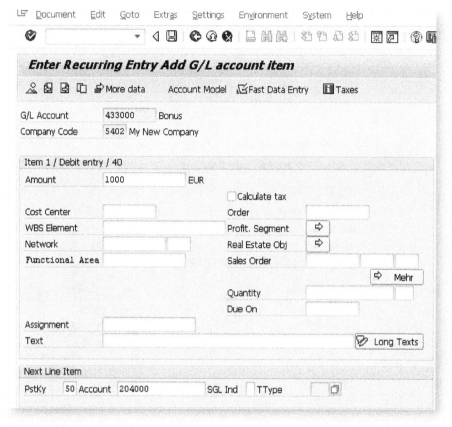

Figure 2.52: Creating a recurring document, step 3

4. Enter the amount for the credit entry (Figure 2.53) and click 💾 to save.

5. The recurring document has now been saved (Figure 2.54):

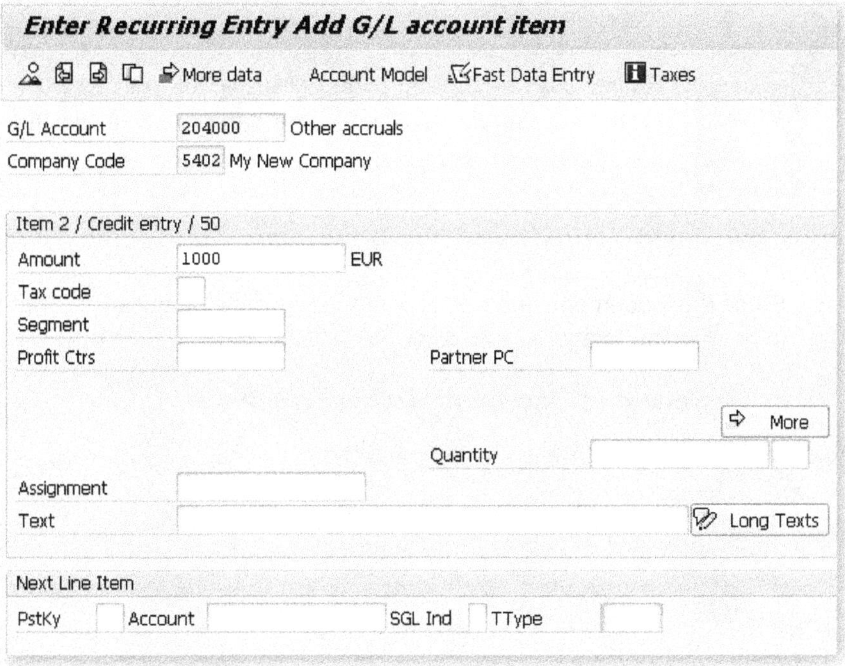

Enter Recurring Entry Add G/L account item

👤 📋 📄 🗐 ➟ More data   Account Model 📝 Fast Data Entry   ℹ️ Taxes

| G/L Account | 204000 | Other accruals |
| Company Code | 5402 | My New Company |

Item 2 / Credit entry / 50

Amount	1000	EUR
Tax code		
Segment		
Profit Ctrs		Partner PC	

➪ More

Quantity

Assignment

Text   📝 Long Texts

Next Line Item

| PstKy | Account | SGL Ind | TType | |

Figure 2.53: Creating a recurring document, step 4

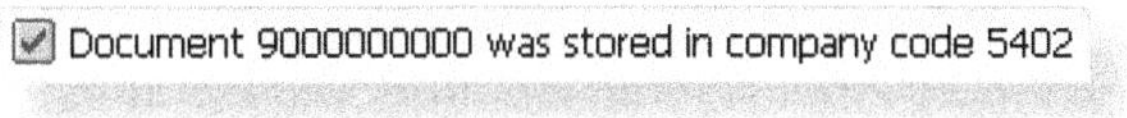

☑ Document 9000000000 was stored in company code 5402

Figure 2.54: Creating a recurring document, step 5

Displaying recurring documents

Now that our recurring document has been posted, each month we can execute transaction F.14 to create a posting. Before we execute the posting, we need to consider the status of our recurring document. Since we created the recurring document with a first run date of 1/1/2014, we must execute the posting first for period 1 and then all subsequent periods up to the current posting period.

To determine which period is next to be processed, we can use transaction FBD3 to display the recurring document.

1. From the SAP Easy Access Menu, navigate to: ACCOUNTING • FINANCIAL ACCOUNTING • GENERAL LEDGER • DOCUMENT • REFERENCE DOCUMENTS • RECURRING DOCUMENT • FBD3 – DISPLAY.

Displaying recurring documents

Rather than navigating to the DISPLAY RECURRING DOC-UMENT screen via the menu, you can type FBD3 in the command field and press Enter to access the screen directly.

2. Enter the document number and company code (Figure 2.55) and click ⊘ in the toolbar at the top of the screen.

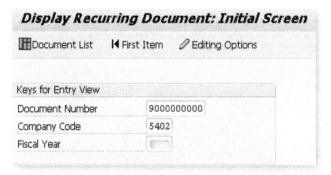

Figure 2.55: Displaying a recurring document, step 2

3. From the toolbar, choose GOTO, RECURRING ENTRY DATA (Figure 2.56).

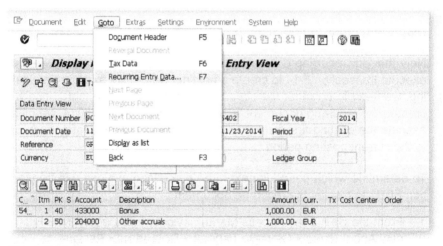

Figure 2.56: Displaying a recurring document, step 3

4. Note that the next run is scheduled for 1/31/2014 (Figure 2.57). This means that to process the recurring entry, it must first be processed for 1/31/2014 unless the recurring document is edited to change the first run date.

Figure 2.57: Displaying a recurring document, step 4

Creating postings for recurring documents

We will now post the recurring document for period 1.

1. From the SAP Easy Access menu navigate to: ACCOUNTING • FINAN-CIAL ACCOUNTING • GENERAL LEDGER • PERIODIC PROCESSING • RE-CURRING ENTRIES • F-14 – EXECUTE.

Posting recurring documents

 Rather than navigating to the recurring entries execution via the menu, you can type F.14 in the command field and press ⌜Enter⌟ to access the recurring entry posting screen directly.

2. Enter selection criteria for our sample document. Note that the settlement period is a required field and must agree with the NEXT RUN ON date shown in Figure 2.57. The recurring document is sent to a batch input session (Figure 2.58).

Create Posting Documents from Recurring Documents

Company code	5402	to	⇨
Document Number	9000000000	to	⇨
Fiscal Year		to	⇨

General selections

Document type		to	⇨
Posting date		to	⇨
Entry date		to	⇨
Reference number		to	⇨
Reference Transaction		to	⇨
Reference key		to	⇨
Logical system		to	⇨

Further selections

Settlement period	01/31/2014	to	⇨
Run schedule		to	⇨
User		to	⇨

Output control

Batch input session name	POSTRECURRNG
User name	CACCIOTTOLLI
Blocking date for BI session	
☐ Hold processed session	

Figure 2.58: Posting a recurring document, step 2

3. The document is output to a batch input session named in the OUT-
    PUT CONTROL section and a confirmation message is issued (Figure
    2.59).

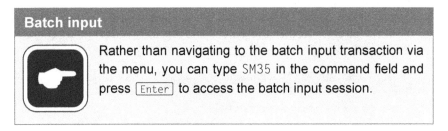

✓ Session POSTRECURRNG was created

Figure 2.59: Posting a recurring document, step 3

4. To process the batch input session, from the SAP Easy Access
    menu, navigate to: TOOLS • ADMINISTRATION • MONITOR • SM35 –
    BATCH INPUT.

> ### Batch input
>
> Rather than navigating to the batch input transaction via
> the menu, you can type SM35 in the command field and
> press [Enter] to access the batch input session.

5. Select the batch input session and choose PROCESS from the menu
    bar (Figure 2.60).

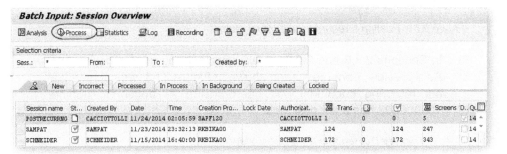

Figure 2.60: Posting a recurring document, step 5

6. Select a processing mode and click PROCESS (Figure 2.61). The
    PROCESS/FOREGROUND option will require you to press [Enter] as
    each screen in the transaction is processed. Selecting DISPLAY ER-
    RORS ONLY will display screens only if errors are encountered. The
    BACKGROUND option does not display any screens as the batch is
    processed. We select DISPLAY ERRORS ONLY so that we can make
    any corrections as the batch is processed.

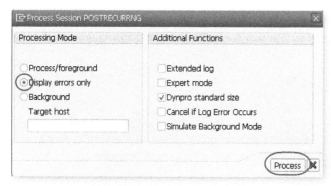

Figure 2.61: Posting a recurring document, step 6

7. With no errors noted in the batch, choose EXIT BATCH INPUT (Figure 2.62).

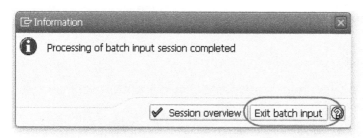

Figure 2.62: Posting a recurring document, step 7

8. In Sections 2.3.6 and 2.3.8 we will review listing posted documents. As a preview, from the screen shown in Figure 2.63, we can see that our recurring document has been posted as document number 100000002 has been assigned.

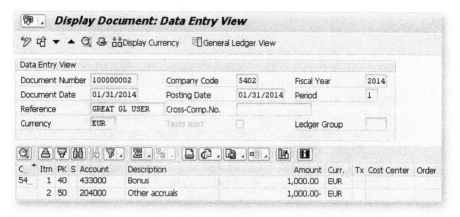

Figure 2.63: Posting a recurring document, step 8

2.3.6 FB03: Displaying G/L account documents

There may be occasions when we want to review a document that we have previously posted. We may or may not know the document number.

1. From the SAP Easy Access menu, navigate to: ACCOUNTING • FINANCIAL ACCOUNTING • GENERAL LEDGER • DOCUMENT • FB03 – DISPLAY.

Displaying accounting documents

 Rather than navigating to the document display transaction via the menu, you can type FB03 in the command field and press Enter to access the document display transaction.

2. Choose DOCUMENT LIST to display a list of documents (Figure 2.64).

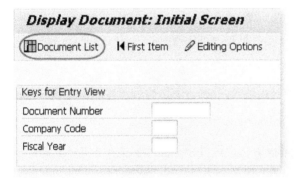

Figure 2.64: Displaying an accounting document, step 2

Displaying accounting documents

 If you know the document number, company code, and fiscal year of the document that you want to display, enter this information in the KEYS FOR ENTRY VIEW fields and press Enter to retrieve the document.

3. Enter filter criteria for selecting documents and click ⊕ to execute (Figure 2.65).

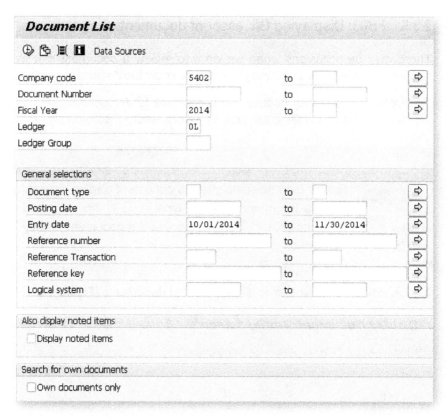

Figure 2.65: Displaying an accounting document, step 3

4. In the list of documents (Figure 2.66), double-click a document or select the document and choose 🔍 to display details.

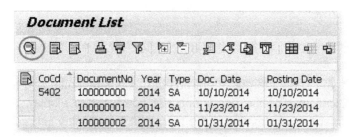

Figure 2.66: Displaying an accounting document, step 4

5. The document is now displayed (Figure 2.67).

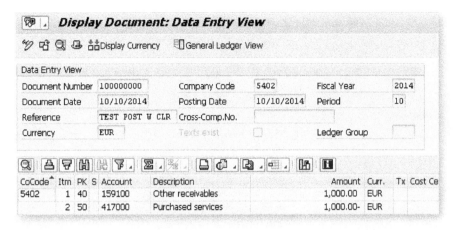

Figure 2.67: Displaying an accounting document, step 5

6. To display the details for any line item, double-click the line or select the line item and click 🔍. The line item details appear (Figure 2.68). Choose the BACK icon ⬅ in the toolbar at the top of the screen to return to the data entry view.

🐘 . Display Document: Line Item 001

🥏 ⬚ 👤 🗎 🗎 🖨 ⬚ Additional Data

G/L Account	159100	Other receivables
Company Code	5402 My New Company	

Doc. no. 100000000

Line Item 1 / Debit entry / 40

Amount	1,000.00	EUR

Additional Account Assignments

Segment		
Profit Ctrs		Partner PC

⇨ More

Value date		Bline Date	🗂
Clearing date	11/23/2014 100000001		
Assignment	20141010		
Text			🐘 Long text

Figure 2.68: Displaying an accounting document, step 6

7. To review header information for the document, click 🗃 (Figure 2.69).

71

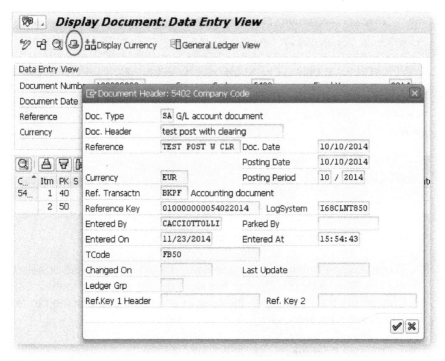

Figure 2.69: Displaying an accounting document, step 7

2.3.7   FB02/FB09: Changing G/L account documents

The ability to change G/L account documents is limited to certain fields such as the assignment, header or line item text, and reference numbers. Amounts in G/L account documents cannot be changed. Let's explore changing both the header and the line item with transaction FB02.

1. From the SAP Easy Access menu, navigate to: ACCOUNTING • FINAN-CIAL ACCOUNTING • GENERAL LEDGER • DOCUMENT • FB02 – CHANGE.

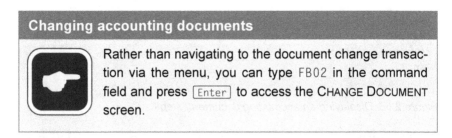

Changing accounting documents

Rather than navigating to the document change transaction via the menu, you can type FB02 in the command field and press ⌈Enter⌉ to access the CHANGE DOCUMENT screen.

2. Enter document 100000000, company code 5402, and fiscal year 2014 and click ✅ to edit our document (Figure 2.70). Alternatively, we could have selected 🏢Document List as shown in Figure 2.64 and then chosen a document to edit from the subsequent list.

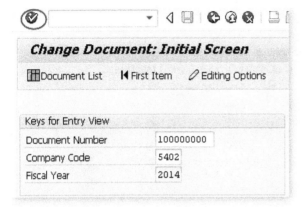

Figure 2.70: Changing an accounting document, step 2

3. Choose 🗔 to change the document header information (Figure 2.71).

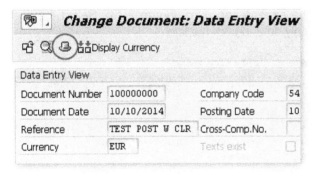

Figure 2.71: Changing an accounting document, step 3

Let's change the reference text. Enter a new text and then click ☑ to continue (Figure 2.72).

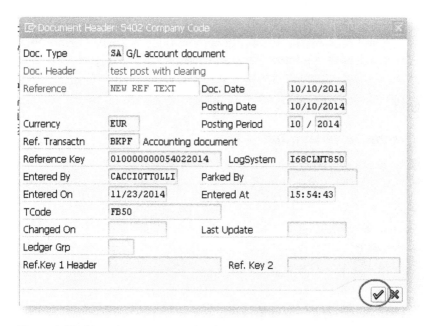

Figure 2.72: Changing an accounting document, step 4

4. Now that the header text has been changed, let's change the text in the line item for the expense account (Figure 2.73). Select the line and click 🔍 or simply double-click the line.

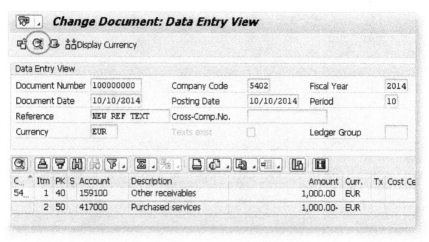

Figure 2.73: Changing an accounting document, step 5

5. Enter the desired changes and click 🖫 to save (Figure 2.74).

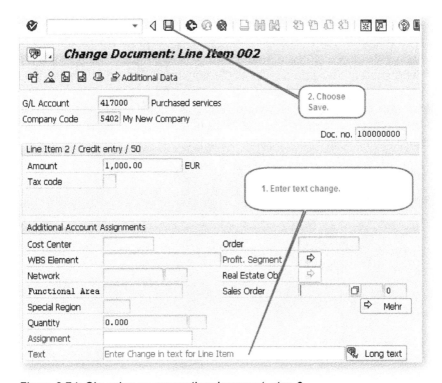

Figure 2.74: Changing an accounting document, step 6

6. A message confirms that changes have been saved (Figure 2.75).

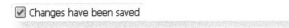

Figure 2.75: Changing an accounting document, step 7

Rather than navigating to the line item from the document header, you can go directly to the line item that is to be changed.

From the SAP Easy Access menu, navigate to: ACCOUNTING • FINANCIAL ACCOUNTING • GENERAL LEDGER • DOCUMENT • FB09 – CHANGE LINE ITEMS.

Changing line items

Rather than navigating to the document change transaction via the menu, you can type FB09 in the command field and press [Enter] to access the CHANGE LINE ITEMS screen directly.

The CHANGE LINE ITEMS screen is similar to the CHANGE DOCUMENT screen (Figure 2.70). You can select ▦Document List to locate documents or we can enter the document details and click ✅ in the toolbar at the top of the screen to navigate directly to the document desired. If the line item is known, it can also be entered. You can also choose to display only line items with specific types of general ledger accounts. This may be useful for G/L account documents with a large number of line items where only a specific type of account requires a change.

Figure 2.76: Displaying/changing line items

2.3.8   FAGLL03: Line item listing

You will often want to list all of the line items for a specific account or group of accounts. From the SAP Easy Access menu, navigate to:

ACCOUNTING • FINANCIAL ACCOUNTING • GENERAL LEDGER • ACCOUNT • FAGLL03 – DISPLAY/CHANGE LINE ITEMS (NEW)

Line item listing	
👉	Rather than navigating to the line item listing via the menu, you can type FAGLL03 in the command field and press Enter to access the screen.

On the selection screen, you can enter the criteria for selecting the line items you wish to display. In the example shown in Figure 2.77, we will request a list of all documents posted to any account within the range of 100000 to 299999 in company code 5402.

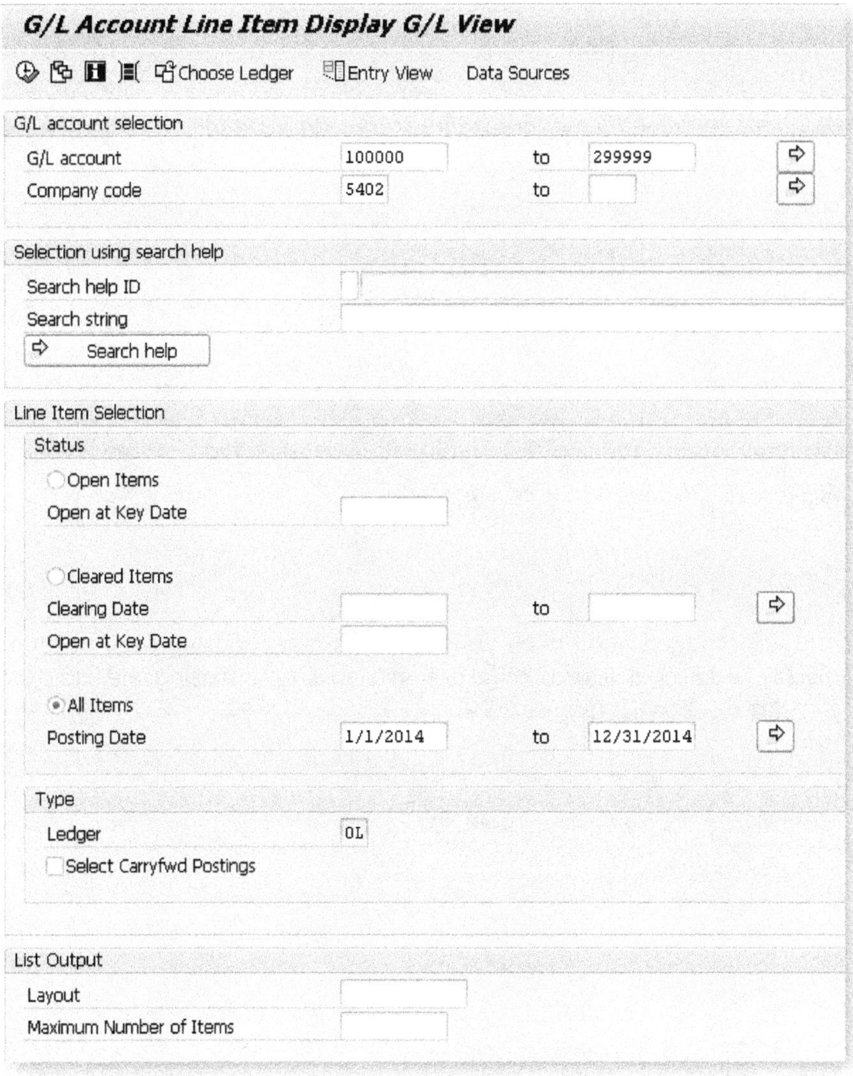

G/L Account Line Item Display G/L View

⊕ ⊡ **H**)⊟(🖵 Choose Ledger   ⊟ Entry View   Data Sources

G/L account selection

G/L account	100000	to	299999	⇨
Company code	5402	to		⇨

Selection using search help

Search help ID	
Search string	
⇨ Search help	

Line Item Selection

Status

○ Open Items
Open at Key Date

○ Cleared Items
Clearing Date   to   ⇨
Open at Key Date

⊙ All Items
Posting Date   1/1/2014   to   12/31/2014   ⇨

Type

Ledger   OL
☐ Select Carryfwd Postings

List Output

Layout	
Maximum Number of Items	

Figure 2.77: G/L account line item display, selecting documents

After entering the selection criteria, click ⊕ to display the list of documents shown in Figure 2.78.

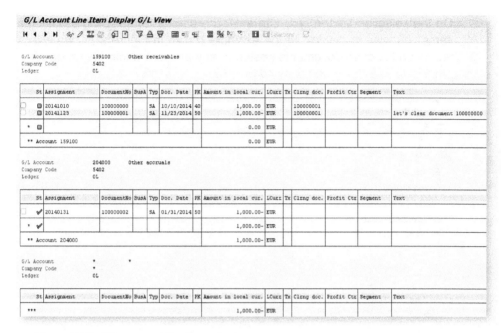

Figure 2.78: G/L account line item display

Custom selections

You may find the need to be very specific when choosing documents to display. Additional filter criteria are available by choosing the CUSTOM SELECTIONS icon]≣[(Figure 2.79).

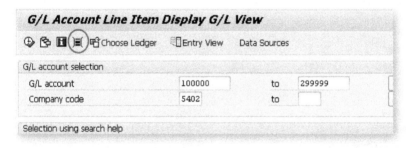

Figure 2.79: Custom selections icon

When you choose this icon a free selection screen appears. The navigation panel on the left contains various characteristics that can be used to further filter the selections. The characteristics are grouped according to categories. Some characteristics pertain to G/L master data, some pertain to the G/L company code, and others pertain to the actual G/L ac-count line items.

When you select characteristics by double-clicking them, they then ap-pear on the right side of the screen in order for you to enter selection criteria. In the example shown in Figure 2.80, only one characteristic (assignment) is chosen; however, you may select many characteristics if desired.

Figure 2.80: Custom selections available

When you have completed the selection, click 🖫 to return to the first screen. You will note that to the right of the custom selection icon there is an indication that one custom selection is active (Figure 2.81):

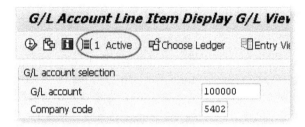

Figure 2.81: Custom selections active

When you choose EXECUTE ⊕, only those documents meeting all filter criteria, including custom selections, are displayed (Figure 2.82).

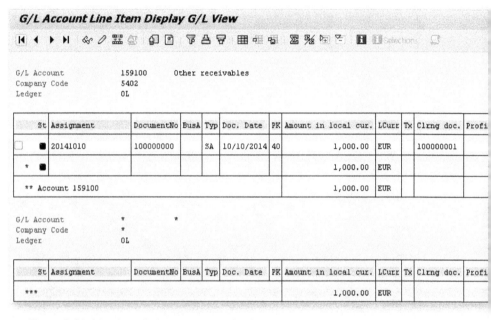

Figure 2.82: Line item listing, custom selections

Creating variants

Now that you have seen the power of custom selections, and have perhaps created a view with multiple criteria, you may be wondering how you will remember all of your choices to repeat the listing in the future. Creating a variant will save you the trouble of remembering, and also of re-entering the criteria.

To save a variant, on the selection screen, with all of your criteria entered, click 🖫 (Figure 2.83).

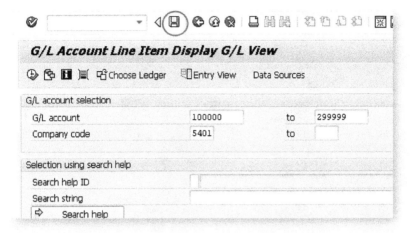

Figure 2.83: Creating a variant

On the VARIANT ATTRIBUTES screen, enter a variant name and description then click 🖫 to save the variant (Figure 2.84).

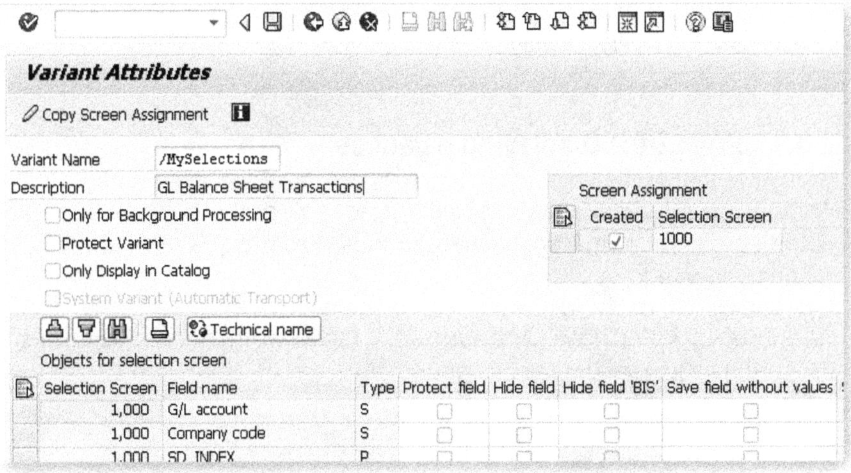

Figure 2.84: Saving the variant name and description

The next time you execute the transaction, click 🔁 to retrieve your variant (Figure 2.85). When the list of variants appears, select your variant and click ✅. Your selection criteria will be populated and you can execute the transaction. You may want to make minor changes to your selection, for example changing a date range, prior to execution.

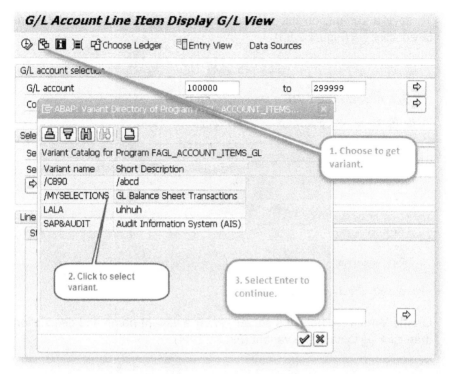

Figure 2.85: Retrieving a variant

2.3.9 FAGLB03: Displaying balances

Another useful transaction enables you to look at the balance in an account across all of the accounting periods. From the SAP Easy Access menu, navigate to:

ACCOUNTING • FINANCIAL ACCOUNTING • GENERAL LEDGER • ACCOUNT • FAGLB03 – DISPLAY BALANCES (NEW)

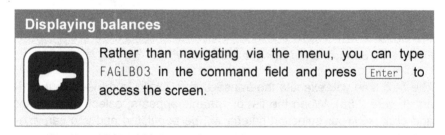

Displaying balances

Rather than navigating via the menu, you can type FAGLB03 in the command field and press [Enter] to access the screen.

Enter selection criteria and click ⊕ to execute (Figure 2.86).

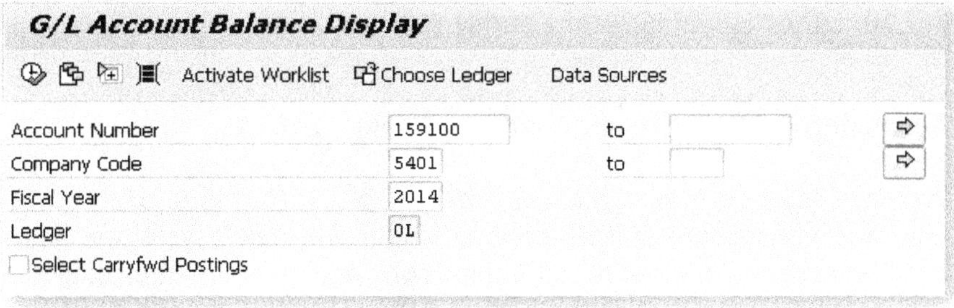

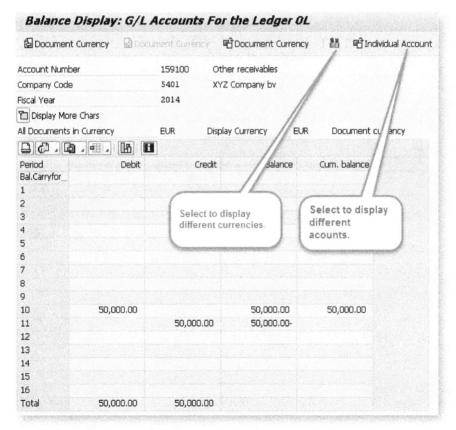

Figure 2.86: Balance display selection criteria

The total debit, total credit, balance, and cumulative balance are shown for each accounting period (Figure 2.87). If you had selected more than one account, you can look at the individual accounts. If your environment is configured for additional currencies (beyond the scope of this book), you can select the currency icon 🛢 to view the various currencies.

Figure 2.87: G/L account balances

2.3.10 Other SAP General Ledger reports

Accessing the SAP G/L Information System

We have seen several transactions that enable us to look at SAP master data and transactions for the general ledger. The SAP system is delivered with dozens of other report transactions and an entire book could be written to cover them. With the basic functions that have been described above for entering selection criteria, using custom selections, and creating variants, you can explore the many reports available to identify reports that fit your needs. The reports are found in the Information System menu. Note that there are various sub-menus where the many reports can be found.

As an example, from the SAP Easy Access menu, navigate to:

ACCOUNTING • FINANCIAL ACCOUNTING • GENERAL LEDGER • INFORMATION SYSTEM • GENERAL LEDGER REPORTS (NEW) • MASTER DATA • S_ALR_87012333 – G/L ACCOUNTS LIST

G/L accounts list

Rather than navigating via the menu, you can type S_ALR_87012333 in the command field and press ⌐Enter⌐ to access the screen.

Although there are many selection options and output formats available, for our example we will simply choose the company code and a table display (Figure 2.88):

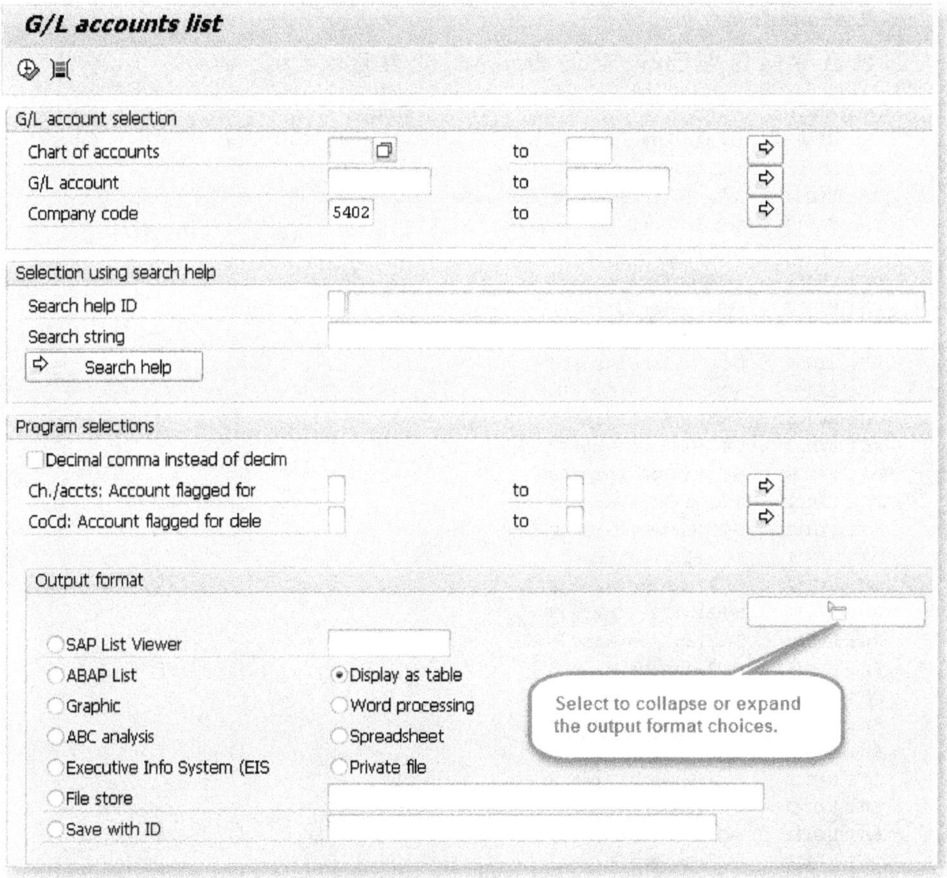

G/L accounts list

⊕ ≣(

G/L account selection

Chart of accounts	☐	to		⇨
G/L account		to		⇨
Company code	5402	to		⇨

Selection using search help

Search help ID	
Search string	
⇨ Search help	

Program selections

☐ Decimal comma instead of decim

Ch./accts: Account flagged for		to		⇨
CoCd: Account flagged for dele		to		⇨

Output format

○ SAP List Viewer

○ ABAP List   ⊙ Display as table

○ Graphic   ○ Word processing

○ ABC analysis   ○ Spreadsheet

○ Executive Info System (EIS   ○ Private file

○ File store

○ Save with ID

Select to collapse or expand the output format choices.

Figure 2.88: G/L accounts list selection

The G/L accounts list is displayed (Figure 2.89).

G/L accounts list

🔊 📇 🖨 🖥 🖲 🖳 🖧 ☷ALV   🖼 📑 📑Extended   📝 🖩 🖩ABC   EIS   Selections

G/L accounts list				Status	/	

ChAc	G/L account	CoCd	Long Text	D D
INT1	100000	5402	Caja Gastos Menores	
INT1	100009	5402	Caja Chica-Entrada de caja deudores(moneda local)	
INT1	100010	5402	Petty cash (with cash journal)	
INT1	100100	5402	Handkasse Gruppe 00	
INT1	100101	5402	Handkasse Gruppe 01	
INT1	100102	5402	Handkasse Gruppe 02	
INT1	100103	5402	Handkasse Gruppe 03	
INT1	100104	5402	Handkasse Gruppe 04	
INT1	100105	5402	Handkasse Gruppe 05	
INT1	100106	5402	Handkasse Gruppe 06	
INT1	100107	5402	Handkasse Gruppe 07	
INT1	100108	5402	Handkasse Gruppe 08	
INT1	100109	5402	Handkasse Gruppe 09	
INT1	100110	5402	Handkasse Gruppe 10	
INT1	100111	5402	Handkasse Gruppe 11	
INT1	100112	5402	Handkasse Gruppe 12	
INT1	100113	5402	Handkasse Gruppe 13	
INT1	100114	5402	Handkasse Gruppe 14	
INT1	100115	5402	Handkasse Gruppe 15	
INT1	100116	5402	Handkasse Gruppe 16	
INT1	100117	5402	Handkasse Gruppe 17	
INT1	100118	5402	Handkasse Gruppe 18	
INT1	100119	5402	Handkasse Gruppe 19	
INT1	100120	5402	Handkasse Gruppe 20	
INT1	100121	5402	Handkasse Gruppe 21	
INT1	100122	5402	Handkasse Gruppe 22	

Figure 2.89: G/L accounts list

This chapter has provided an overview of SAP General Ledger. Using this book as a guide, you should be able to create basic master data and transactions in the general ledger.

2.4 Exercises

2.4.1 Add a G/L account (expense account)

Account #	474272
Description	Travel costs, auto tolls
Group account number	312400
Field status group	G069

Table 2.3: Details for the new G/L account

2.4.2 Post an entry to include the new expense account

Debit account 474272, EUR 50
Credit account 165099, EUR 50

Hint

You may need to use transaction OB52 to insure that posting periods for the company codes posting period variant of 1000 are open, as shown in Figure 2.90.

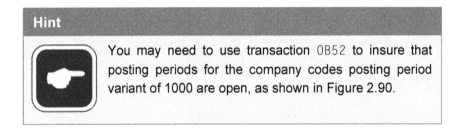

Figure 2.90: OB52 – posting periods

2.4.3 Add an open item G/L account

Account: 159105 – Employee Receivables
Description: Employee Receivables
Sort key: 001
Group account: 125300
Field status group: G019

2.4.4 Post an entry to the new open item account

Amount of entry: 1000 debit
Currency: EUR
Offset to account: 474250

Attention	
	Use transaction FS00 to check that the control data does not have a tax category, and that posting without tax is allowed.

2.4.5 Post with clearing to clear the item posted above

Charge off the open item to account 110000.

2.4.6 Display documents posted

3 Getting started with SAP Accounts Receivable

This chapter includes a discussion of the configuration and master data required for managing accounts receivable. You will also be introduced to some of the transaction codes for creating postings to customer accounts, including invoices and credit memos. You will learn how to apply customer payments in order to clear open receivable items. The chapter also looks at some of the reports available for accounts receivable.

3.1 What is SAP Accounts Receivable (AR)?

In our discussion of accounting at the beginning of Chapter 2, we learned about general ledger accounts which enable a business to record business transactions in order to present reports on the business activity in a *profit & loss* or *P&L* report, or to present the net worth of a business in a *balance sheet* report.

When the accounting transaction involves a customer, for example, an invoice sent to the customer for a sales transaction, the general ledger account transaction is recorded as a debit to an accounts receivable account and a credit to a revenue account.

In order for the business to follow up on accounts receivable transactions and collect from its customers, the accounting system must provide a significant amount of information for each of the accounting transactions related to customers. For example, the terms of the customer invoice, which indicate a due date and any available discount that might be available to the customer when remitting payment, are important to enable an accounts receivable clerk to know when to follow up on outstanding customer invoices. Other information, such as the customer address and contact information, is also important for following up on outstanding receivable transactions.

In the chapter on the general ledger we saw that the master data for general ledger accounts does not contain any of the aforementioned information. To enable detailed reporting of accounts receivable, a *sub-*

sidiary ledger (generally referred to as a *subledger*) containing all of the details specific to receivable accounts but not needed in general ledger accounts is used.

The subsidiary ledger total will agree to the total in the general ledger account for accounts receivable. The general ledger account is known as the control account or reconciliation account.

It is the integration functionality of the SAP system that keeps the control account synchronized with the subledger account. There are other accounting systems where this is not the case and separate posting and reconciliation activity is required.

Similar to the design of the general ledger, in the SAP Accounts Receivable module we have master data and transaction data. (Refer to Section 2.1 for a refresher on the definitions of master data and transaction data).

3.2   Customer master data

3.2.1   Customer master records

In our introduction to SAP Accounts Receivable (AR), we mentioned that there is a significant amount of information that can be maintained for customers to facilitate collection and reporting. Many of the fields are used in SAP modules that integrate with AR, such as SD (Sales and Distribution) or FSCM (Financial Supply Chain Management). Because a discussion of all of the options is beyond the scope of this book, in this section, as we create a customer, we will utilize only a few of the numerous fields available.

1.   From the SAP Easy Access menu, navigate to: ACCOUNTING • FINANCIAL ACCOUNTING • ACCOUNTS RECEIVABLE • MASTER RECORDS • FD01 - CREATE.

Creating customer master records

 Rather than navigating via the menu, you can type FD01 in the command field and press [Enter] to access the CUSTOMER CREATE: INITIAL SCREEN.

2. On the CUSTOMER CREATE: INITIAL SCREEN (Figure 3.1), we have the option to create an account with reference to other accounts; however, in our case we will create a new customer from scratch. Use the dropdown option for the ACCOUNT GROUP field to select the STANDARD CUSTOMER account group. Enter the company code and click ✅ to continue. In our IDES environment, the STANDARD CUSTOMER account group has been configured for automatic assignment of customer numbers, therefore the customer field is left blank.

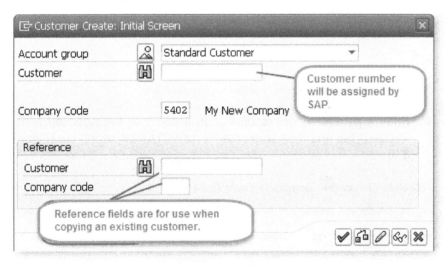

Figure 3.1: Creating a customer master record, step 2

3. Enter the customer name and address information on the ADDRESS tab. Select [Company Code Data] (Figure 3.2).

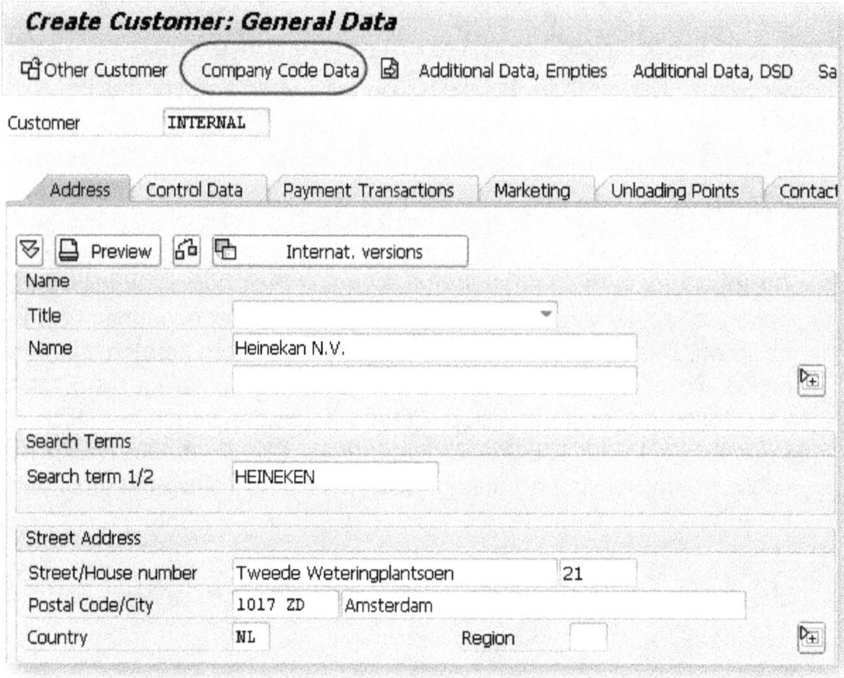

Figure 3.2: Creating a customer master record, step 3

4. Enter a general ledger reconciliation account on the ACCOUNT MAN-
    AGEMENT tab and then select the PAYMENT TRANSACTIONS tab (Figure
    3.3).

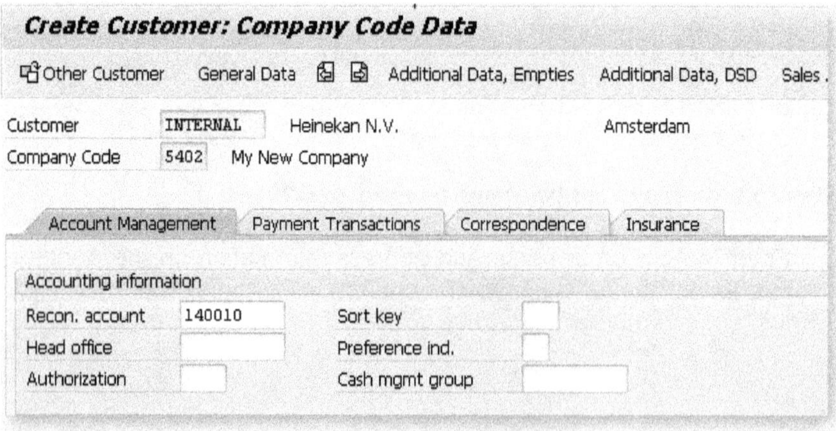

Figure 3.3: Creating a customer master record, step 4

5. Enter a code for the terms of payment and then click 🖫 in the toolbar at the top of the screen to save (Figure 3.4).

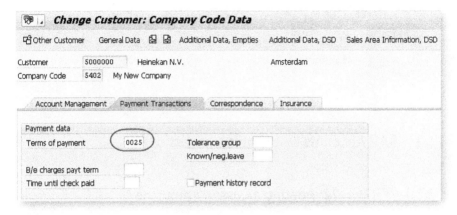

Figure 3.4: Creating a customer master record, step 5

6. Because we did not save the general data prior to entering company code data, we need to confirm the general data. Click ✔ to continue (Figure 3.5).

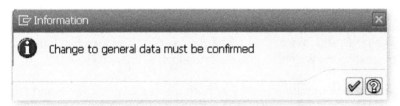

Figure 3.5: Creating a customer master record, step 6

7. The SAP system returns a message confirming that the customer record has been created (Figure 3.6).

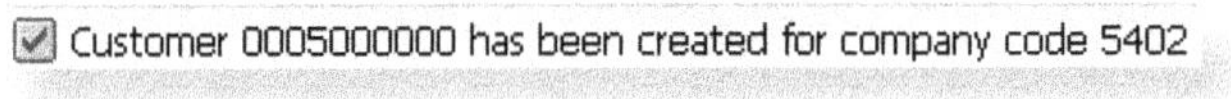

☑ Customer 0005000000 has been created for company code 5402

Figure 3.6: Creating a customer master record, step 7

The new customer is now available for posting.

How do I display or change an existing customer master record?

 To display an existing customer record, use transaction FD03. To change an existing customer record, use transaction FD02.

3.3 SAP Accounts Receivable transactions

3.3.1 FB70/F-22: Posting a customer invoice

With a customer master record created, we can use SAP transactions to post invoices to the customer account.

You may recall from the discussion of double-entry accounting in Section 1.2 that each accounting document contains equal and offsetting debits and credits. When we record a customer invoice to charge a customer, we create a debit entry to the customer account and a credit entry (typically) to a profit and loss account. The SAP system provides two transactions for posting invoices to customer accounts: FB70 and F-22.

Both transactions require the entry of both the customer account and the offsetting profit and loss account(s), and both transactions produce the same result in the accounting records. However, the entry screens are different. The screen layout of FB70 is conducive to posting to one customer. F-22 can be used to post one invoice to multiple customers or to post entries to more than one company code. In addition, the currency rate for invoices in foreign currencies can be input manually with F-22.

Let's post an invoice using each of the transactions.

Transaction FB70: Invoice

In this example, we will post a customer invoice to one customer with a single line item posting to one profit and loss account to offset the account receivable.

1. From the SAP Easy Access menu, navigate to: ACCOUNTING • FINAN-CIAL ACCOUNTING • ACCOUNTS RECEIVABLE • DOCUMENT ENTRY • FB70 – INVOICE.

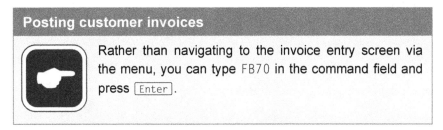

Posting customer invoices

Rather than navigating to the invoice entry screen via the menu, you can type `FB70` in the command field and press `Enter`.

Figure 3.7: Posting a customer invoice, FB70, step 1

2. From the toolbar, select ⬚ Company Code . Enter the company code and then click ✅ to continue (Figure 3.8).

Figure 3.8: Posting a customer invoice, FB70, step 2

3. Enter details for the document as shown in Figure 3.9. Press `Enter` to navigate past any warning messages related to posting periods, for example: ⚠ Period 12 adjusted in line with posting date 09/05/2014 .

In Figure 3.9, the fields in which information was entered are highlighted. In addition to entering an invoice amount, note that the G/L account that offsets the invoice must be entered in the item section below. The base-line date and payment terms code are entered on the PAYMENT tab. Click 💾 in the toolbar at the top of the screen to save the entries.

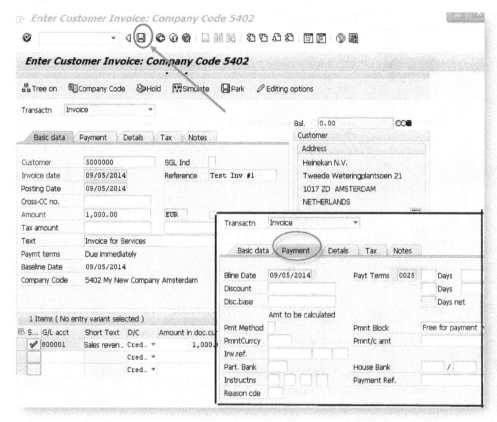

Figure 3.9: Posting a customer invoice, FB70, step 3

G/L account for offset

> Be sure to choose an offset G/L account that does not require a tax category, as we have not configured taxes in our sample environment. Use transaction FS00 to display the account and then select the CONTROL DATA tab and make sure that the tax category field is empty.

4. If desired, use transaction FB03 (as described in Section 2.3.6) to display the document (Figure 3.10):

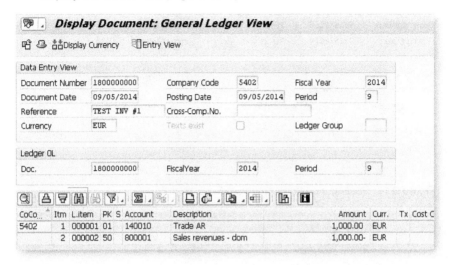

Figure 3.10: Posting a customer invoice, FB70, step 4

Transaction F-22: Invoice – General

In this example, we will post a customer invoice that charges two different customers and also has multiple offsetting profit and loss accounts.

1. From the SAP Easy Access menu, navigate to: ACCOUNTING • FINANCIAL ACCOUNTING • ACCOUNTS RECEIVABLE • DOCUMENT ENTRY • F-22 INVOICE – GENERAL.

Posting customer invoices

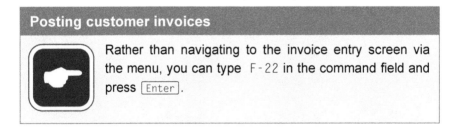

Rather than navigating to the invoice entry screen via the menu, you can type F-22 in the command field and press [Enter].

2. Enter details for the document as shown in Figure 3.11 and press [Enter]. The fields in which information was entered for our example are highlighted:

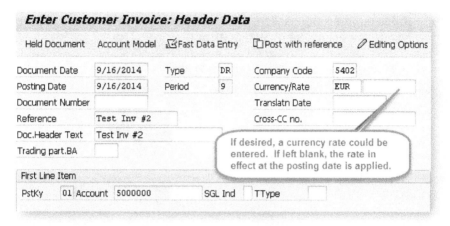

Figure 3.11: Posting a customer invoice, F-22, step 2

Posting keys

F-22 requires us to enter or select posting keys. The posting key for a customer invoice is 01. The posting key for a credit to a general ledger account is 50. To display available posting keys, press F4 when your cursor is in the POSTING KEY field.

3. On the next screen (Figure 3.12) we enter the invoice amount and payment terms. At the bottom of the screen we enter the second customer to be included in the invoice document. Press Enter to navigate past any warning messages related to posting periods, payment terms, or due dates.

Enter Customer invoice: Add Customer item

👤 🗄 🗃 🗇 ⮂ More data   Account Model 📇 Fast Data Entry   ⓘ Taxes

Customer	5000000	Heinekan N.V.	G/L Acc	140010
Company Code	5402	Tweede Weteringplantsoen 21		
My New Company		Amsterdam		

Item 1 / Invoice / 01

Amount	3500	EUR	
Tax amount			
	☐ Calculate tax	Tax code	**
Contract	/	Flow Type	
Bus. Area			
Payt Terms	0025	Days/percent	/ /
Bline Date	09/16/2014	Disc. amount	
Disc. base		Invoice ref.	/ /
Pmnt Block		Pmt Method	
Payment cur.		Pmnt/c amnt	
Payment Ref.			
Assignment			
Text			✏ Long Texts

Next line item

PstKy	01	Account	5000005	SGL Ind	TType	New co.code	

Figure 3.12: Posting customer invoice, F-22, step 3

4. On the next screen (Figure 3.13), we enter the details for the second customer. At the bottom of the screen we can enter a customer or we can enter posting key 50 and begin the entry of the profit and loss offset account(s). We can also take advantage of the FAST DATA EN-TRY option at the top of the screen. Rather than entering the next line item, click 📇 Fast Data Entry .

Enter Customer invoice: Add G/L account items

👤 🗐 🗐 🗖 ✍More data   Account Model ✍Fast Data Entry ℹ️ Taxes

Customer	5000005	Grolsch Brewery	G/L Acc	140010
Company Code	5402	Browerslaan 1		
My New Company		Enschede		

Item 2 / Invoice / 01

Amount	2000	EUR		
			Tax code	**
Contract		/	Flow Type	
Bus. Area				
Payt Terms	0025		Days/percent	/ /
Bline Date	09/16/2014		Disc. amount	
Disc. base			Invoice ref.	/ /
Pmnt Block			Pmt Method	
Payment cur.			Pmnt/c amnt	
Payment Ref.				
Assignment				
Text				🗭 Long Texts

Next line item

PstKy		Account	SGL Ind	TType		New co.code

Figure 3.13: Posting customer invoice, F-22, step 4

5. Enter the line item details for the offsetting profit and loss accounts and click 🖫 to post the entry (Figure 3.14).

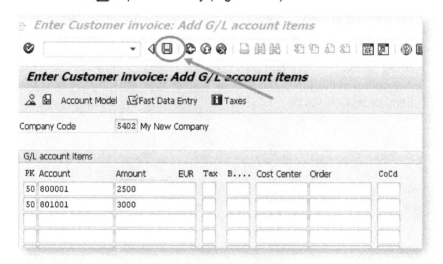

Figure 3.14: Posting a customer invoice, F-22, Step 5

6. If desired, use transaction FB03 (as described in Section 2.3.6) to display the document (Figure 3.15).

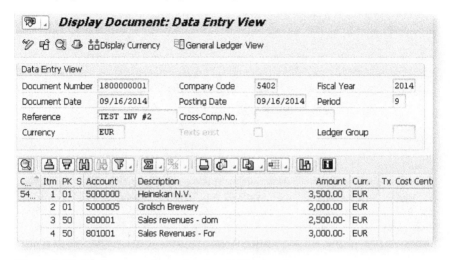

Figure 3.15: Posting a customer invoice, F-22, step 6

3.3.2   FB75/F-27: Posting a credit memo

When we record a customer credit memo to credit a customer, we create a credit entry to the customer account and a debit entry (typically) to a profit and loss account. Similar to the situation for posting customer invoices, the SAP system provides two transactions for posting credits to customer accounts: FB75 and F-27.

Transaction FB75: Credit Memo

1. From the SAP Easy Access menu, navigate to: ACCOUNTING • FINANCIAL ACCOUNTING • ACCOUNTS RECEIVABLE • DOCUMENT ENTRY • FB75 - CREDIT MEMO.

> **Posting customer credit memos**
>
> Rather than navigating to the credit memo entry screen via the menu, you can type FB75 in the command field and press [Enter].

2. Enter details for the document as shown in Figure 3.16 and then click 🖫. The fields in which information was entered for our example are highlighted:

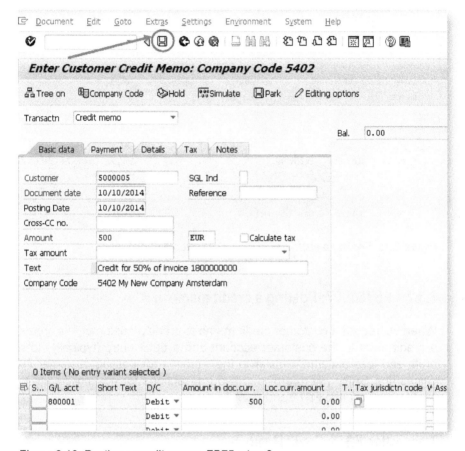

Figure 3.16: Posting a credit memo, FB75, step 2

3. If desired, use transaction FB03 (as described in Section 2.3.6) to display the document (Figure 3.17):

Display Document: General Ledger View

Display Currency ☑️Entry View

Data Entry View

Document Number	1600000000	Company Code	5402	Fiscal Year	2014
Document Date	10/10/2014	Posting Date	10/10/2014	Period	10
Reference		Cross-Comp.No.			
Currency	EUR	Texts exist ☐		Ledger Group	

Ledger OL

Doc.	1600000000	FiscalYear	2014	Period	10

C...	Itm	L.item	PK	S	Account	Description	Amount	Curr.	Tx	Cost
54...	1	000001	11		140010	Trade AR	500.00-	EUR		
	2	000002	40		800001	Sales revenues - dom	500.00	EUR		

Figure 3.17: Posting a credit memo, FB75, step 3

Transaction F-27: Credit Memo – General

1. From the SAP Easy Access menu, navigate to: ACCOUNTING • FINAN-CIAL ACCOUNTING • ACCOUNTS RECEIVABLE • DOCUMENT ENTRY • F-27 CREDIT MEMO – GENERAL.

2. Enter details for the document as shown in Figure 3.18 and then press ⌊Enter⌋.

Enter Customer Credit Memo: Header Data

Held Document   Account Model   ☑️Fast Data Entry   ⎙Post with reference   ⊘ Editing Options

Document Date	10/15/2014	Type	DG	Company Code	5402
Posting Date	10/15/2014	Period	10	Currency/Rate	EUR
Document Number				Translatn Date	
Reference	Test CR #2			Cross-CC no.	
Doc.Header Text	Test CR #2				
Trading part.BA					

First Line Item

PstKy	11	Account	5000000	SGL Ind	TType	

Figure 3.18: Posting a credit memo, F-27, step 2

Posting keys

 F-27 requires us to enter or select posting keys. The posting key for a customer credit memo is 11. The posting key for a credit to a general ledger account is 40. To display available posting keys, press ⌨F4⌨ when your cursor is in the POSTING KEY field.

---

3. Press ⌨Enter⌨ to navigate past any warning messages related to posting periods, payment terms, or due dates, for example:
    ⚠ Period 01 adjusted in line with posting date 10/10/2014

4. Enter the credit memo amount and payment terms. At the bottom of the screen, enter the posting key and offsetting general ledger account for the credit memo (Figure 3.19):

Enter Customer credit memo: Add Customer item

👤 🗂 🗐 🗋 ⮕More data   Account Model   ☑Fast Data Entry   🛈 Taxes

Customer	5000000 Heinekan N.V.	G/L Acc 140010
Company Code	5402 Tweede Weteringplantsoen 21	
My New Company	Amsterdam	

Item 1 / Credit memo / 11

Amount	300 EUR	
Tax amount		
	☐ Calculate tax	Tax code **
Contract	/	Flow Type
Bus. Area		
Payt Terms	0025	Days/percent / /
Bline Date	10/15/2014	Disc. amount
Disc. base		Invoice ref. / /
Pmnt Block		Pmt Method
Payment cur.		Pmnt/c amnt
Assignment		
Text		🗟 Long Texts

Next line item

PstKy 40 Account 800001   SGL Ind   New co.code

Figure 3.19: Posting a credit memo, step 4

5. Press ⌈Enter⌋ to navigate past any warning messages related to posting periods, payment terms, or due dates, for example:
⚠ Net due date on 11/15/2014 is in the past

6. Enter the amount for the general ledger offset and click 🖫 to post the credit memo (Figure 3.20).

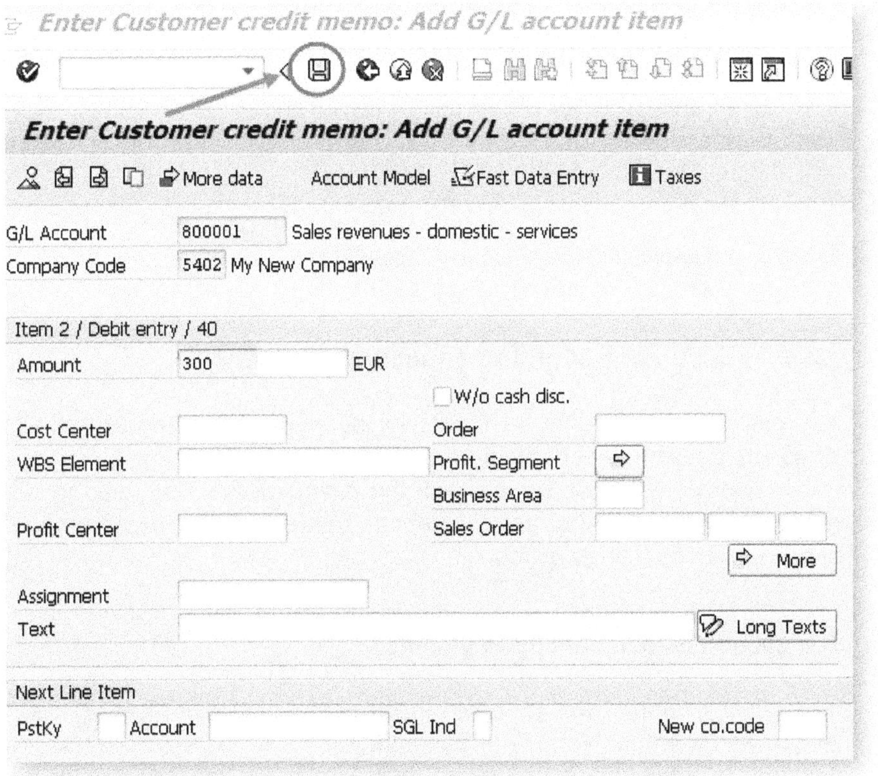

Figure 3.20: Posting a credit memo, F-27, step 6

7. Use FB03 (as described in Section 2.3.6) to display the document if desired (Figure 3.21):

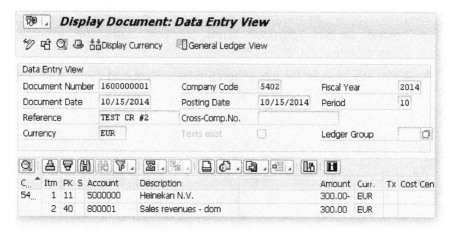

Figure 3.21: Posting a credit memo, F-27, step 7

3.3.3   F-28/F-26: Recording an incoming payment

The process of recording payments for customer invoices has several steps. In addition to entering the payment amount, we must choose which invoices we want to clear with the payment. We also need to determine the disposition of any differences between the payment amount and the invoices being cleared.

Transaction F-28: Incoming Payments

In our first example, we will enter a payment which will offset an open invoice and a credit memo. The payment will not be enough to offset the documents — the difference will be less than the tolerance amount we defined for our customers. We will let the SAP system automatically charge off the difference to the account defined in the account determination configuration.

1.   From the SAP Easy Access menu, navigate to: ACCOUNTING • FINANCIAL ACCOUNTING • ACCOUNTS RECEIVABLE • DOCUMENT ENTRY • F-28 – INCOMING PAYMENTS.

Posting incoming payments

Rather than navigating to the incoming payments entry screen via the menu, you can type F-28 in the command field and press [Enter].

2. Enter the basic information about the payment as shown below and then select Process Open Items (Figure 3.22).

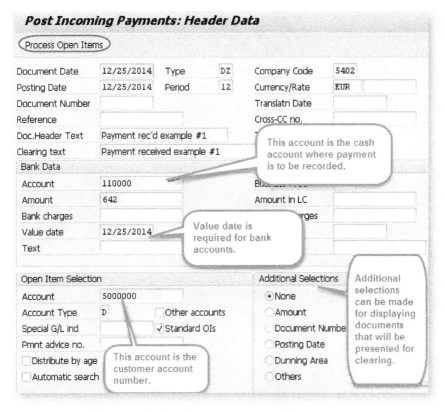

Figure 3.22: Posting incoming payments, F-28, step 2

3. Because we did not choose any specific selection criteria on the previous screen, we are presented with all of the documents that are open for our customer. In Figure 3.23, you will note that these items total much more than our payment amount of 642.00. We can also see that the 5% discount which was applicable to the credit memo on the account is automatically reflected. However, the 5% discount on the invoice is not reflected since the discount amount is only available if the payment is received within 5 days of the invoice date.

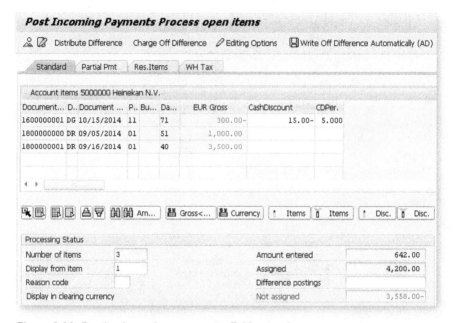

Figure 3.23: Posting incoming payments, F-28, step 3

4. In our example, we will assume that the customer's remittance advice indicated that payment is being made for document 1800000000 and the customer is deducting the credit document 1600000001. In addition, the customer is taking the full 5% discount even though he is not paying within the terms specified. Due to our relationship with the customer, we will allow the discount despite the late payment.

First we must exclude invoice 1800000001 from the list. Position your cursor on this document that is not being paid and click ⎓ Items to deactivate the item (Figure 3.24).

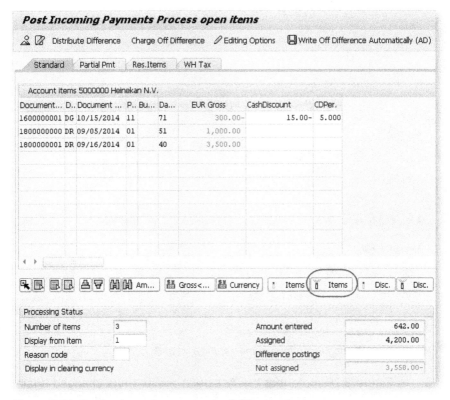

Figure 3.24: Posting incoming payments, F-28, step 4

5. Note that document 1800000001 is no longer included in the items to be cleared with the payment (see Figure 3.25); the amount is in a black font. In addition, the ASSIGNED and NOT ASSIGNED amounts have changed. Now enter the discount percentage and press ⎡Enter⎤ (Figure 3.25).

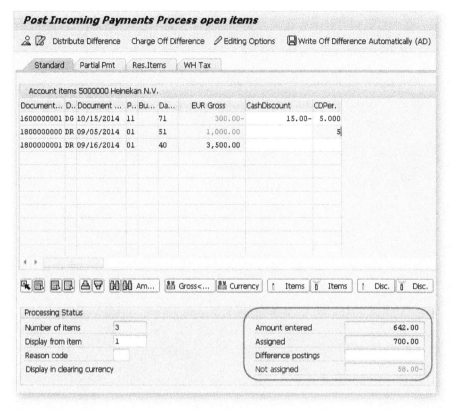

Figure 3.25: Posting incoming payments, F-28, step 5

6. In Figure 3.26, note that the ASSIGNED amount has changed again. Click 🖫 to post the payment and have the 8.00 unassigned amount charged off to the configured tolerance account.

7. Use transaction FB03 (as described in Section 2.3.6) to display the document if desired. In Figure 3.27, note that the discount amount and tolerance amount have been charged to the accounts configured for automatic account determination (Customer discounts and Other sales deductions).

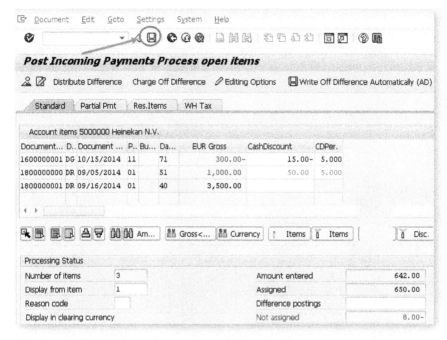

Figure 3.26: Posting incoming payments, F-28, step 6

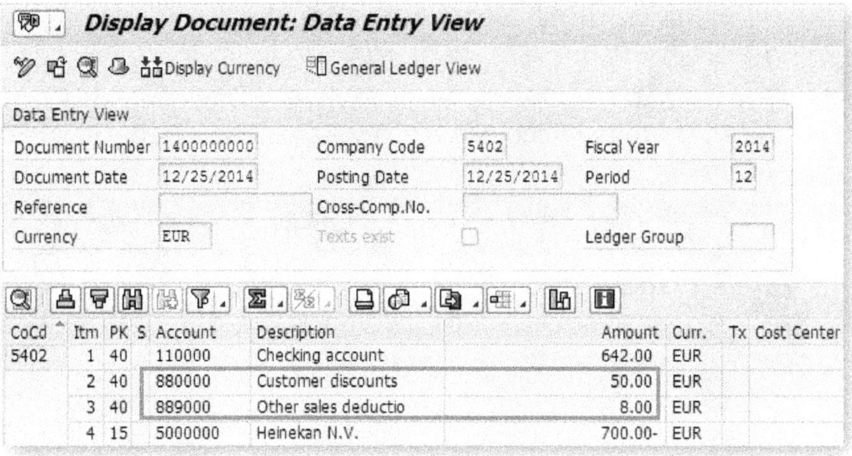

Figure 3.27: Posting incoming payments, F-28, step 7

Transaction F-26: Payment Fast Entry

Just as we have seen with transaction F-28, the fast entry function posts a payment document to the customer's account and allows us to clear open items.

Before we demonstrate using transaction F-26, let's use transaction FBL5N to take a look at the open items for customer 5000005 (Figure 3.28). Section 3.4.1 provides a detailed explanation for using FBL5N.

Customer	5000005
Company Code	5402
Name	Grolsch Brewery
City	Enschede

	Stat	Type	Doc. Date	Net due dt	Clearing	Amt in loc.cur.	LCurr	DocumentNo
☐	☒	DR	10/01/2014	11/30/2014		4,000.00	EUR	1800000002
☐	☒	DR	10/01/2014	11/30/2014		5,000.00	EUR	1800000003
*	☒					9,000.00	EUR	
** Account 5000005						9,000.00	EUR	

Figure 3.28: Open items for a customer

For our example, we will record a payment of 4000 to clear invoice 1800000002.

1. From the SAP Easy Access menu, navigate to: ACCOUNTING • FINAN-CIAL ACCOUNTING • ACCOUNTS RECEIVABLE • ENTRY • F-26 – PAYMENT FAST ENTRY.

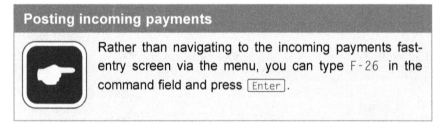

Posting incoming payments

Rather than navigating to the incoming payments fast-entry screen via the menu, you can type F-26 in the command field and press ⌈Enter⌉.

2. Enter the header information and choose ENTER PAYMENTS (Figure 3.29).

Incoming Payments Fast Entry: Header Data

🗑 Delete   📇   📇 (Enter Payments)

Specifications for the following incoming payments

Company Code	5402	Document Type	DZ
Posting Date	12/25/2014	Posting Period	4
Bank account	110000		
Business Area	🔍	Trading part.BA	🔍
Profit Center	🔍		
Special G/L ind.			

Default data for the following incoming payments

Currency	EUR
Reference	
Document Date	12/25/2014
Value date	

Additional input fields	Additional selections
☐ Reference number	☐ Amount
☐ Bank charges	☐ Pmnt advice no.
☐ Clearing text	☐ Selection by date
☐ Automatic allocation procedure	☑ Selection by customer/vendor ref.key
☐ Document header text	

Figure 3.29: Posting incoming payments, F-26, step 2

3. Enter payment information, including document 1800000002, and select PROCESS OPEN ITEMS (Figure 3.30)

Incoming Payments Fast Entry

👤 (Process Open Items) Further Selections   Specifications

Company code	5402	My New Company
Bank account	110000	Checking account

Payment details

Customer	5000005		Document Date	12/25/2014
Amount	4000	EUR	Amount in LC	
			Value date	12/25/2014

Line items paid

Doc./reference	Reference key
1800000002	

Figure 3.30: Posting incoming payments, F-26, step 3

4. Select 🖫 to post the payment.

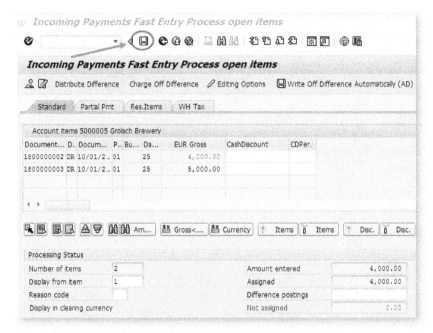

Figure 3.31: Posting incoming payments, F-26, step 4

5. Use transaction FB03 (as described in Section 2.3.6) to display the posted payment if desired (Figure 3.32).

Figure 3.32: Posting incoming payments, F-26, step 5

3.3.4   Parking customer documents

Similar to parking for general ledger documents, which was described in Section 2.3.3, customer documents can be entered and not posted and instead parked for subsequent posting. Just as we had several options for posting invoices and credit memos, we have several options for parking documents. After a document is parked, it can be posted with the same FBV0 transaction demonstrated for parked general ledger documents and illustrated in Figure 2.37 through Figure 2.41.

We will explore transaction FV70 – Park/Edit Invoice in the steps below.

1. From the SAP Easy Access menu, navigate to: ACCOUNTING • FINAN-CIAL ACCOUNTING • ACCOUNTS RECEIVABLE • DOCUMENT ENTRY • DOC-UMENT PARKING • FV70 – PARK/EDIT INVOICE.

Parking customer documents

 Rather than navigating to the entry screen for parking customer documents via the menu, you can type `FV70` in the command field and press `Enter`.

---

2. Enter details for the document then choose ⊟ Save as completed (Figure 3.33).

3. Note that the document has been parked:
   ☑ Document 1800000005 5402 was parked

4. To post the invoice, follow the steps as described in Section 2.3.3 FV50/FV50L: Parked documents. Use transaction FBV0 and enter the document number, or use the document list function to locate the document (Figure 3.34).

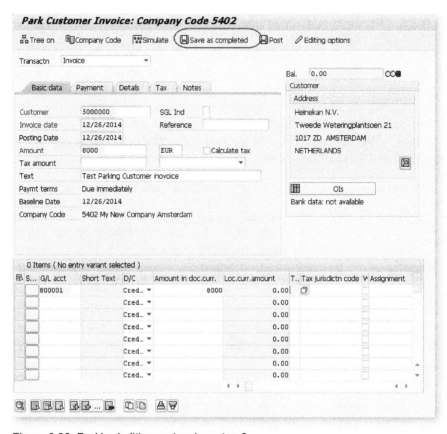

Figure 3.33: Parking/editing an invoice, step 2

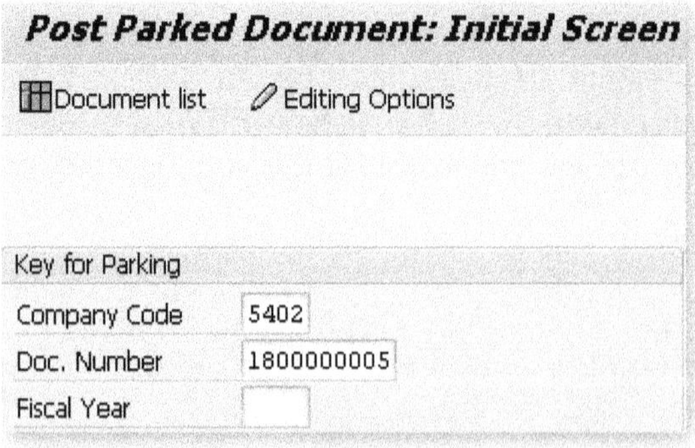

Post Parked Document: Initial Screen

Document list   Editing Options

Key for Parking

Company Code	5402
Doc. Number	1800000005
Fiscal Year	

Figure 3.34: Parking/editing an invoice, step 4

5. On the parked document editing screen click Post (Figure 3.35).

Figure 3.35: Parking/editing an invoice, step 5

6. Use transaction FB03 (as described in Section 2.3.6) to display the document if desired (Figure 3.36).

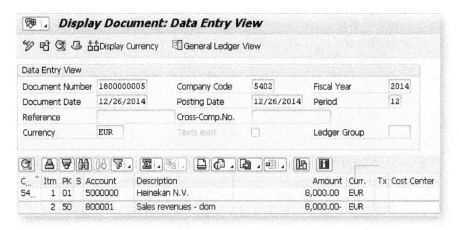

Figure 3.36: Parking/editing an invoice, step 6

3.4   SAP Accounts Receivable (AR) reports

SAP provides dozens of reports for analyzing customer accounts. Just as we noted in our discussion of general ledger reports, an entire book could be dedicated solely to accounts receivable reports in SAP. I will cover a few of the most common reports and encourage you to explore the AR Information System to learn the power and flexibility that comes with SAP.

3.4.1 Displaying customer balances

1. To display customer balances, from the SAP Easy Access menu, navigate to: ACCOUNTING • FINANCIAL ACCOUNTING • ACCOUNTS RE-CEIVABLE • ACCOUNT • FD10N - DISPLAY BALANCES.

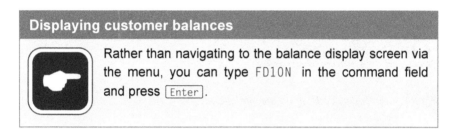

Displaying customer balances

Rather than navigating to the balance display screen via the menu, you can type FD10N in the command field and press [Enter].

2. Enter a customer number, company code, and fiscal year and then click ⊕ (Figure 3.37).

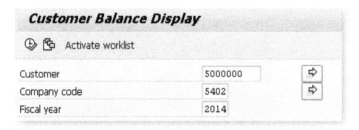

Customer Balance Display

⊕ 🔁 Activate worklist

Customer	5000000	⇨
Company code	5402	⇨
Fiscal year	2014	

Figure 3.37: Displaying customer balances, step 2

3. Customer balances are displayed by fiscal period (Figure 3.38). You can double-click an amount to display the detailed line items.

4. Detailed line items are displayed (Figure 3.39).

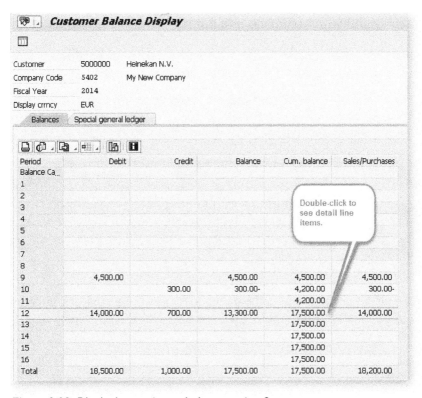

Customer Balance Display

Customer	5000000	Heinekan N.V.	
Company Code	5402	My New Company	
Fiscal Year	2014		
Display crrncy	EUR		

Balances | Special general ledger

Period	Debit	Credit	Balance	Cum. balance	Sales/Purchases
Balance Ca...					
1					
2					
3					
4					
5					
6					
7					
8					
9	4,500.00		4,500.00	4,500.00	4,500.00
10		300.00	300.00-	4,200.00	300.00-
11				4,200.00	
12	14,000.00	700.00	13,300.00	17,500.00	14,000.00
13				17,500.00	
14				17,500.00	
15				17,500.00	
16				17,500.00	
Total	18,500.00	1,000.00	17,500.00	17,500.00	18,200.00

> Double-click to see detail line items.

Figure 3.38: Displaying customer balances, step 3

Customer Line Item Display

Customer		5000000		
Company Code		5402		
Name		Heinekan N.V.		
City		Amsterdam		

	Stat	Type	Doc. Date	Net due dt	Clearing	Amt in loc.cur.	LCurr	DocumentNo
☐	◉	DR	09/16/2014	11/15/2014		3,500.00	EUR	1800000001
☐	◉	DR	12/26/2014	12/26/2014		6,000.00	EUR	1800000004
☐	◉	DR	12/26/2014	12/26/2014		8,000.00	EUR	1800000005
*	◉					17,500.00	EUR	
☐	◻	DZ	12/25/2014	12/25/2014	12/25/2014	700.00-	EUR	1400000000
☐	◻	DG	10/15/2014	10/15/2014	12/25/2014	300.00-	EUR	1600000001
☐	◻	DR	09/05/2014	11/04/2014	12/25/2014	1,000.00	EUR	1800000000
*	◻					0.00	EUR	
	** Account 5000000					17,500.00	EUR	

Figure 3.39: Displaying customer balances, step 4

3.4.2 Displaying customer line items

Rather than navigating to line items from the customer balance display, you can use the line item display transaction.

1. From the SAP Easy Access menu, navigate to: ACCOUNTING • FINAN-CIAL ACCOUNTING • ACCOUNTS RECEIVABLE • ACCOUNT • FBL5N – DIS-PLAY/CHANGE LINE ITEMS.

Displaying customer line items	
	Rather than navigating to the screen for displaying customer line items via the menu, you can type `FBL5N` in the command field and press Enter .

2. Enter an account and company code. Choose the type of line items to be displayed. In Figure 3.40, we have chosen to display all line items posted for customer 5000005.

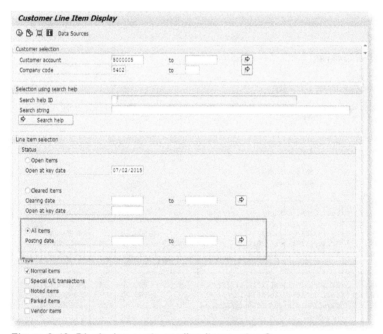

Figure 3.40: Displaying customer line items, step 2

3. Customer line items are displayed (Figure 3.41).

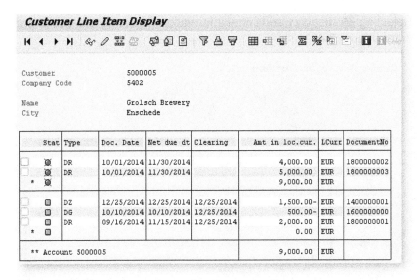

Figure 3.41: Displaying customer line items, step 3

4. To display details, double-click a line item. In Figure 3.42, note that for the document we selected, 1800000001, we can see details such as the payment terms and the clearing document—the DZ payment document that was recorded to when the customer paid the invoice.

Figure 3.42 Displaying customer line items, step 4

5. Selecting 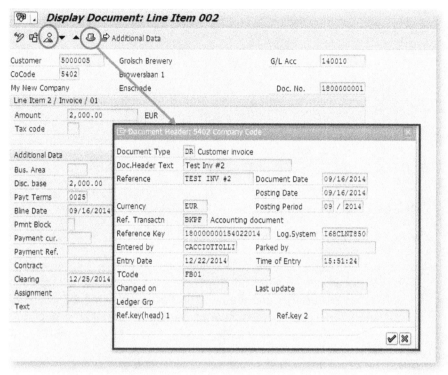 displays additional information regarding the document entry (Figure 3.43).

Figure 3.43: Displaying customer line items, step 5

6. Selecting the document overview icon ⚙ (Figure 3.43) displays the document entry view similar to the view for transaction FB03 (Figure 3.44).

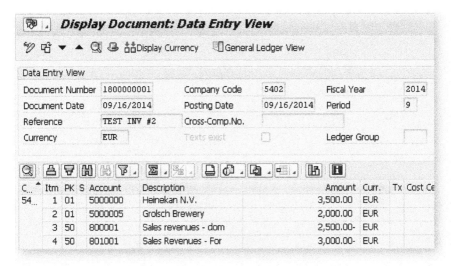

Figure 3.44: Displaying customer line items, step 6

3.4.3 Accessing the SAP Accounts Receivable Information System

As noted previously, many reports are delivered with the SAP system. In this section, we will demonstrate one of the reports and how you can use layouts to create customized views. The techniques can be applied to many of the SAP reports, providing great flexibility in getting information out of the system.

To access the many reports, from the SAP Easy Access menu, navigate to the Accounts Receivable Information System:

ACCOUNTING • FINANCIAL ACCOUNTING • ACCOUNTS RECEIVABLE • INFORMATION SYSTEM • REPORTS FOR ACCOUNTS RECEIVABLE ACCOUNTING

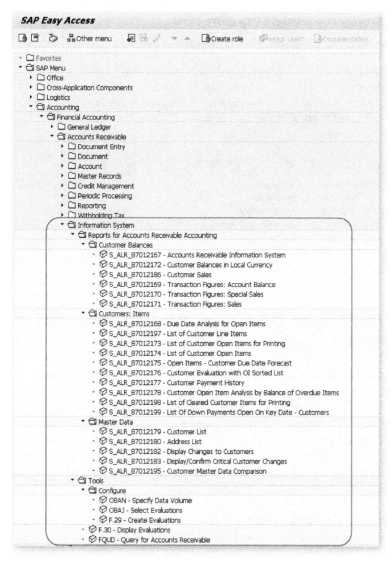

Figure 3.45: Accounts Receivable Information System

Customer open item report

A common business practice is to analyze open items based on their due date, categorizing the outstanding balances of invoices according to how many days they are past their due date. Let's take a look at an open item analysis report that summarizes the open accounts receivable in aging categories.

1. Select report S_ALR_87012173 from the SAP Easy Access menu by double-clicking it.

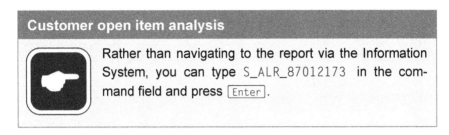

2. Enter selection criteria and click ⏱ to execute (Figure 3.46).

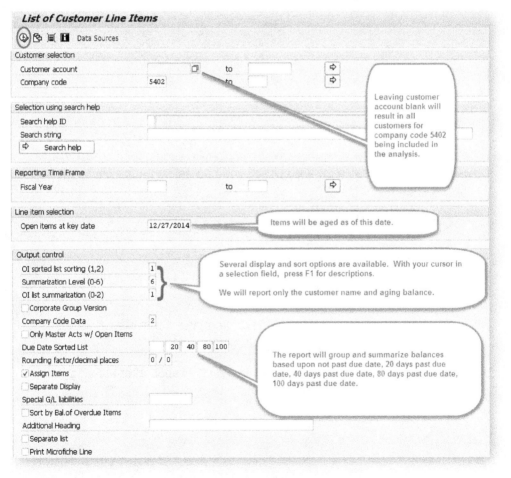

Figure 3.46: Customer open items report, step 2

3. The report is returned (Figure 3.47):

Customer Open Item Analysis by Balance of Overdue Items

My New Company — Customer Open Item Analysis by Balance of Overdue Items — Time 02:22:04 — Date 12/27/2014
Amsterdam — RFDOPR10/CACCIOTTOLLI Page — 1

Company code 5402 Accounting clerk, Key date 12/27/14 Amounts in EUR

Customer Number	Sorting Field	Coun	OI Total	From 0 To 0	From 1 To 20	From 21 To 40	From 41 To 80	From 81 To 100	From 101
0005000000 HEINEKEN		NL	17,500		14,000		3,500		
0005000005 GROLSCH		NL	9,000			9,000			

My New Company — Customer Open Item Analysis by Balance of Overdue Items — Time 02:22:04 — Date 12/27/2014
Amsterdam — RFDOPR10/CACCIOTTOLLI Page — 2

Totals Sheet: Company Code 5402 Clerk, Key date 12/27/14 Amounts in EUR

BusAr Curr-ency	Down Payt	OI Total	Typ	From 0 To 0	From 1 To 20	From 21 To 40	From 41 To 80	From 81 To 100	From 101
**	0	26,500	Ove		14,000	9,000	3,500		
** Ann. Sales/Pur.: LC							28,700.00		

Figure 3.47: Customer open items report, step 3

Creating a report layout

You may observe that for many of the delivered reports, the OUTPUT VARIANTS section contains an area where you can select and/or configure a layout (Figure 3.48).

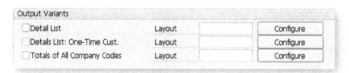

Figure 3.48: Report layout selections

Let's choose report S_ALR_87012172 from the CUSTOMER BALANCES section of the Accounts Receivable Information System.

Before we create a layout, let's execute (⊕) the report after entering the selection criteria shown in Figure 3.49.

Customer Balances in Local Currency

Customer selection

Customer account		to		⇨
Company code	5402	to		⇨

Selection using search help

Search help ID	
Search string	
⇨ Search help	

Reporting Time Frame

Fiscal Year	2014	to		⇨

Further selections

Reporting Periods	1	to	16	
Reconciliation Account		to		⇨
Account Balance		to		⇨
Special G/L Indicator		to		⇨

Output control

- ☐ Corporate Group Version
- ☑ Normal Balances
- ☐ Special G/L Balances
- ☐ Drill down one-time accounts
- ☐ Accounts Not Posted To
- ☐ Only customers with cred.bal.
- ☑ Customer's Address
- ☐ List separation
- ☐ Microfiche Line
- Additional Heading
- ☐ Keep Print Parameters for Output

Output Variants

☑ Detail List	Layout		Configure	
☐ Details List: One-Time Cust.	Layout		Configure	
☐ Totals of All Company Codes	Layout		Configure	

Figure 3.49: Selection criteria for customer balances report

Note in Figure 3.50 that this default view does not show the customer's full name; only the search term for the customer is displayed. In addition, we can see several amount fields.

Customer Balances in Local Currency

My New Company			Customer Balances in Local Currency				Time 00:14:33	Date 12/28/2014
Amsterdam							RFDSLD00/CACCIOTTOLLI Page	1

Carryforwd Perio 00 - 00 2014 Reporting Period 01 - 16 2014

CoCd Reconciliation acct Customer	SearchTerm SGL Ind. Crcy	Balance Carryforward	Debit rept.period	Credit report per.	Accumulated balance
5402 140010 5000000	HEINEKEN EUR	0.00	18,500.00	1,000.00	17,500.00
5402 140010 5000005	GROLSCH EUR	0.00	11,000.00	2,000.00	9,000.00
* 5402 140010	EUR	0.00	29,500.00	3,000.00	26,500.00
** 5402	EUR	0.00	29,500.00	3,000.00	26,500.00
***	EUR	0.00	29,500.00	3,000.00	26,500.00

Figure 3.50: Customer balance report default view

Let's create a layout that will show the customer's name and only the accumulated balance.

1. Select ⬚ Configure ⬚ in the OUTPUT VARIANTS section of the selection screen (Figure 3.51).

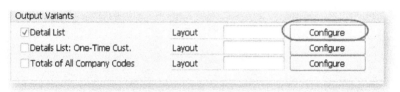

Figure 3.51: Configuring the report layout, step 1

2. From the layout display, choose ▦ to change the layout (Figure 3.52).

Customer Balances in Local Currency

CoCd Reconciliation acct Customer	SearchTerm SGL Ind. Crcy	Balance Carryforward	Debit rept.period	Credit report per.	Accumulated balance
XXXX XXXXXXXXXX	XXXXXXXXXX XXXXXXXXXX X XXXXX	0.00	0.00	0.00	0.00
XXXX XXXXXXXXXX	XXXXXXXXXX XXXXXXXXXX X XXXXX	0.00	0.00	0.00	0.00
XXXX XXXXXXXXXX	XXXXXXXXXX XXXXXXXXXX X XXXXX	0.00	0.00	0.00	0.00
* XXXX XXXXXXXXXX	XXXXX	0.00	0.00	0.00	0.00
** XXXX	XXXXX	0.00	0.00	0.00	0.00
***	XXXXX	0.00	0.00	0.00	0.00

Figure 3.52: Configuring the report layout, step 2

3. From the panel on the left, select the fields that we wish to remove from the report and then click ▶ to move them to the panel on the right (Figure 3.53).

4. Select the NAME field in the panel on the right. Then choose the position in the panel on the left where this field should appear. Choose ◀ to move the field across (Figure 3.54).

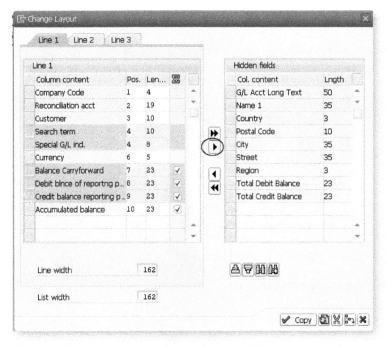

Figure 3.53: Configuring the report layout, step 3

Figure 3.54: Configuring the report layout, step 4

5. Select the copy button ✓ Copy and note the new layout (Figure 3.55).

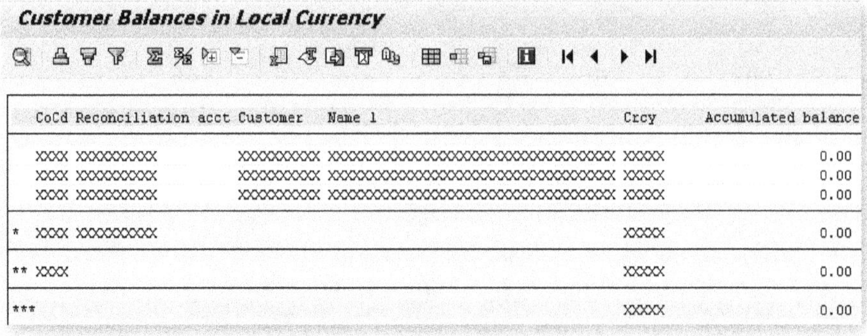

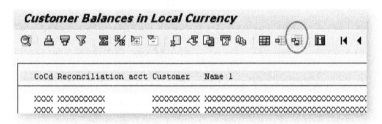

Figure 3.55: Configuring the report layout, step 5

6. Select 🖫 to save the layout (Figure 3.56).

Figure 3.56: Configuring the report layout, step 6

7. Give the layout a name and description and then click ✓ Save (Figure 3.57). If USER-SPECIFIC is selected, only you will be able to use the layout. You may need to obtain authorizations in order to save layouts that can be shared.

Layout	MYLAYOUT	✓ User-specific
Description	My New Report Layout	

Subobjects

✓ Sort criteria

✓ Subtotal criteria

   Expansion to sum. level   0   Non-total lines

✓ Save ✗

Figure 3.57: Configuring the report layout, step 7

130

8. Choose ⚙ in the toolbar at the top of the screen to return to the report selection screen. Now, in the OUTPUT VARIANTS section, select the dropdown icon ⬚ to the right of the LAYOUT field (or use F4) to display a list of available layouts (Figure 3.58).

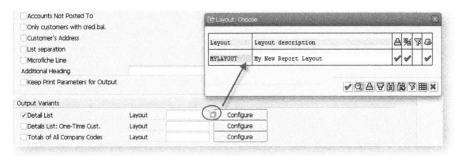

Figure 3.58: Configuring the report layout, step 8

9. Double-click MYLAYOUT so that it appears in the LAYOUT selection field and then click ⚙ to execute the report (Figure 3.59).

Output Variants			
✓ Detail List	Layout	MYLAYOUT	Configure
Details List: One-Time Cust.	Layout		Configure
Totals of All Company Codes	Layout		Configure

Figure 3.59: Configuring the report layout, step 9

10. Note the new layout displayed (Figure 3.60).

Customer Balances in Local Currency

My New Company   Customer Balances in Local Currency   Time 01:30:27   Date 12/28/2014
Amsterdam   RFDSLD00/CACCIOTTOLLI Page   1
Carryforwd Perio 00 - 00 2014 Reporting Period 01 - 16 2014

CoCd Reconciliation acct Customer	Name 1	Crcy	Accumulated balance
5402 140010 5000000	Heinekan N.V.	EUR	17,500.00
5402 140010 5000005	Grolsch Brewery	EUR	9,000.00
* 5402 140010		EUR	26,500.00
** 5402		EUR	26,500.00
***		EUR	26,500.00

Figure 3.60: Configuring the report layout, step 10

Report layouts

Whenever the change layout icon ⊞ is available you can change the layout of a report and save it for future use. This applies to all SAP reports.

3.5 Exercises

3.5.1 Create a customer

Account group	0004 – Special Customers
Customer info	Deventer Zutphenseweg 51 7418 AH Deventer Netherlands
Reconciliation account	140010

3.5.2 Post two customer invoices

Customer	Deventer
Invoice #1 info Date Reference Amount GL offset	 Today's date New invoice 1 EUR 1000 800001
Invoice #2 info Date Reference Amount GL offset	 Today's date New invoice 2 EUR 15000 800001

3.5.3 Post a payment receipt for one of the customer invoices created

Document date	Today's date
Document type	DZ
Currency	EUR
Bank account	110000
Payment amount	EUR 1000

3.5.4 Display open items with standard reports/transaction codes

4 Getting started with SAP Accounts Payable

This chapter includes a discussion of the configuration and master data required for managing accounts payable. You will also be introduced to some of the transaction codes for managing postings to vendor accounts and making payments to vendors. The chapter also looks at some of the reports available for accounts payable.

4.1 What is SAP Accounts Payable (AP)?

Most business enterprises make many purchases of goods and services daily from many vendors. Payments to the vendors are rarely made at the time of purchase. Based on agreements with the vendors, payments may be made some time after the purchase; for example, within 30 days. In addition, the payment amount may also vary: for example, the terms of payment may state that if the company pays the vendor within 10 days, they may deduct 1% discount.

The SAP Accounts Payable module enables a company to record the expenses when incurred, monitor and settle the liabilities resulting from expenses, and facilitate the company's ability to take advantage of any discounts offered by vendors.

An SAP accounting transaction involving a purchase to be paid at a later date is recorded as a debit to an expense account and a credit to an accounts payable account. Similar to the discussion about SAP Accounts Receivable in the previous chapter, SAP Accounts Payable represents a *subledger* containing all details specific to payable accounts. Through the integration features of SAP, the subsidiary ledger will always agree to the total in the general ledger.

4.2 Vendor master data

Creating vendor master records

In our introduction to SAP Accounts Payable, we noted that a significant amount of detail may be maintained for vendor master records. For example, in addition to address information, our vendor master record can include information about the vendor's bank account, tax numbers, and payment terms. If your environment is integrated with SAP's Materials Management module, there may be many screens required related to processing purchase orders and invoices. Make sure you collaborate with members of the procurement organization. In the master records we create here, we will focus only on those items necessary to post accounts payable documents such as vendor invoices and check payments. Let's create a vendor master record in our sample company code.

1. From the SAP Easy Access menu, navigate to: ACCOUNTING • FINANCIAL ACCOUNTING • ACCOUNTS PAYABLE • MASTER RECORDS • FK01 – CREATE.

Creating vendor master records

 Rather than navigating via the menu, you can type FK01 in the command field and press ⌈Enter⌉ to access the CREATE VENDOR: INITIAL SCREEN.

---

2. On the CREATE VENDOR: INITIAL SCREEN, we have the option to create an account with reference to other accounts; however, in our case, we will create a new vendor record from scratch. Enter a company code, use the dropdown list to select the DOMESTIC VENDORS (NL) group and then select ENTER ✅ (Figure 4.1).

3. Enter the vendor name and address information and then choose 🔜 (Figure 4.2) to move forward through the screens until the ACCOUNTING INFORMATION screen appears.

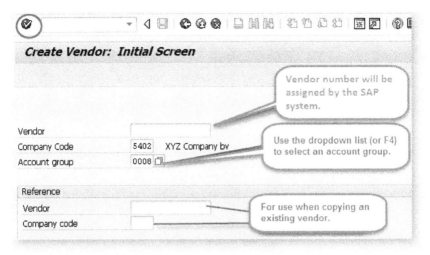

Figure 4.1: Creating a vendor master record, step 2

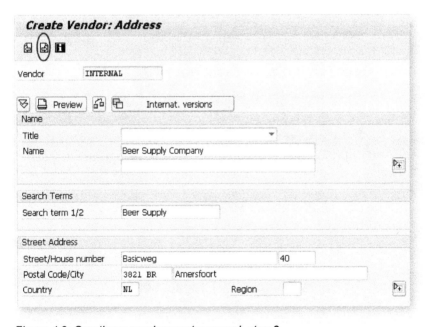

Figure 4.2: Creating a vendor master record, step 3

4. Enter a reconciliation account and then move forward through the screens again until the PAYMENT TRANSACTIONS ACCOUNTING screen appears (Figure 4.3). Enter C for check payment (or any other desired payment method) and click 🖫 to save the entries.

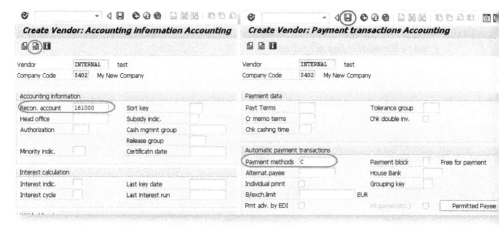

Figure 4.3: Creating a vendor master record, step 4

5. The SAP system issues a message stating that the vendor record has been created.

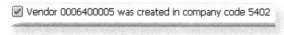

Vendor 0006400005 was created in company code 5402

Figure 4.4: Creating a vendor master record, step 5

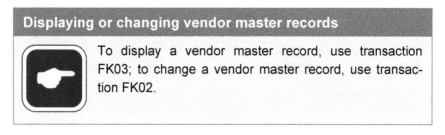

Displaying or changing vendor master records

To display a vendor master record, use transaction FK03; to change a vendor master record, use transaction FK02.

The new vendor is now available for posting.

4.3 SAP Accounts Payable (AP) transactions

There are many ways that AP transactions can be entered in the SAP system. In many instances, invoices are processed through the Materials Management (MM) module and actually involve a series of documents including a purchase order, a goods receipt (GR) document, and an invoice receipt (IR) document. The configuration and functionality of MM is beyond the scope of this book, so we will focus on vendor invoices without a purchase order that are entered directly into the SAP system.

4.3.1 FB60/F-43: Posting a vendor invoice

With a vendor master record created, we can now use SAP transactions to post invoices to the vendor account.

You may recall from the discussion of double-entry accounting in Section 1.2 that each accounting document contains equal and offsetting debits and credits. When we record a vendor invoice, we create a debit entry (typically) to a profit and loss account and a credit entry to the vendor account. The SAP system provides two transactions for posting invoices to vendor accounts: FB60 and F-43.

Both transactions require the entry of both the vendor account and the offsetting profit and loss account(s), and both transactions produce the same result in the accounting records; however, the entry screens are different. The screen layout of FB60 is conducive to posting to one vendor. F-43 can be used to post one invoice to multiple vendors or to post entries to more than one company code. In addition, the currency rate for invoices in foreign currencies can be input manually with F-43.

Let's post an invoice using each of the transactions.

Transaction FB60: Invoice

In this example we will post a vendor invoice to one vendor with a single line item posting to one profit and loss account to offset the account payable.

1. From the SAP Easy Access menu, navigate to: ACCOUNTING • FINANCIAL ACCOUNTING • ACCOUNTS PAYABLE • DOCUMENT ENTRY • FB60 – INVOICE.

Posting vendor invoices

 Rather than navigating to the invoice entry screen via the menu, you can type FB60 in the command field and press ⌈Enter⌋.

---

2. From the toolbar, select ⊞Company Code , enter the company code for posting, and then click ✅ to continue (Figure 4.5).

Figure 4.5: Posting a vendor invoice, FB60, step 2

3. Enter details for the document as shown in Figure 4.6. Press `Enter` to navigate past any warning messages related to posting periods, for example: ⚠ Period 01 adjusted in line with posting date 10/10/2014

The fields in which information was entered are highlighted. In addition to entering an invoice amount, note that the G/L account that offsets the invoice must be entered in the item section below. We had not specified any terms on our vendor master file so the default for the invoice will be due immediately. If desired, a baseline date and payment terms can be entered on the PAYMENT tab. We will assume the invoice is due immediately and no terms need to be entered. Click 💾 to save the entries.

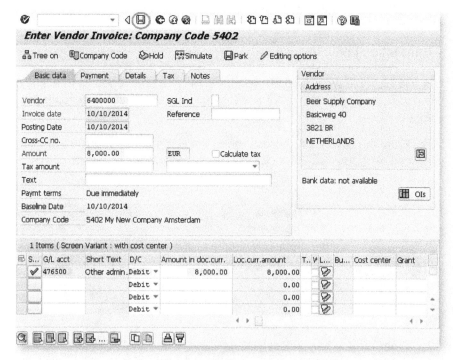

Figure 4.6: Posting a vendor invoice, FB60, step 3

G/L account for offset

 Be sure to choose an offset G/L account that does not require a tax category, as we have not configured taxes in our sample environment. Use transaction FS00 to display the account and select the CONTROL DATA tab and make sure that the tax category field is empty.

4. If desired, use transaction FB03 (as described in Section 2.3.6) to display the document (Figure 4.7).

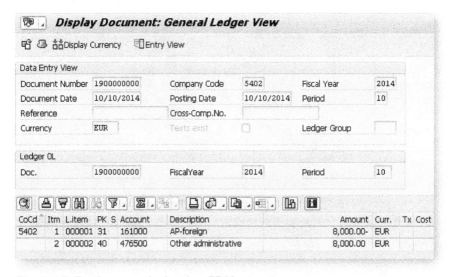

Figure 4.7: Posting a vendor invoice, FB60, step 4

Transaction F-43 – Invoice – General

In this example, we will post an accounts payable document that will be split between two different vendors and also has multiple offsetting profit and loss accounts.

1. From the SAP Easy Access menu, navigate to: ACCOUNTING • FINANCIAL ACCOUNTING • ACCOUNTS PAYABLE • DOCUMENT ENTRY • F-43 INVOICE – GENERAL.

Posting vendor invoices

 Rather than navigating to the invoice entry screen via the menu, you can type F-43 in the command field and press Enter.

2. Enter details for the document as shown in Figure 4.8 and press Enter. The fields in which information was entered for our example are highlighted. Press Enter to navigate past any warning messages related to posting periods, payment terms, or due dates.

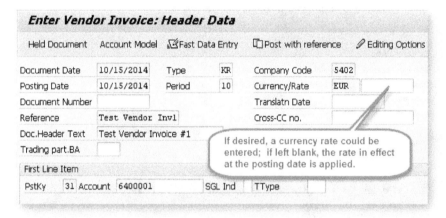

Figure 4.8: Posting a vendor invoice, F-43, step 2

Posting keys

 F-43 requires us to enter or select posting keys. The posting key for a vendor invoice is 31. The posting key for a debit to a general ledger account is 40. To display available posting keys, press F4 when your cursor is in the POSTING KEY field.

3. On the next screen we enter the invoice amount and payment terms (Figure 4.9). At the bottom of the screen we enter the second vendor to be included in the invoice document.

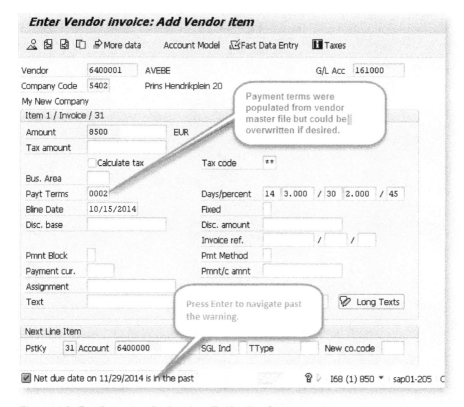

Figure 4.9: Posting a vendor invoice, F-43, step 3

4. On the next screen, we enter the details for the second vendor (Figure 4.10). At the bottom of the screen we can enter the vendor, or we can enter posting key 40 and begin the entry of the profit and loss offset account(s). We can also take advantage of the FAST DATA ENTRY option at the top of the screen. Rather than entering the next line item, click ⟨Fast Data Entry⟩ .

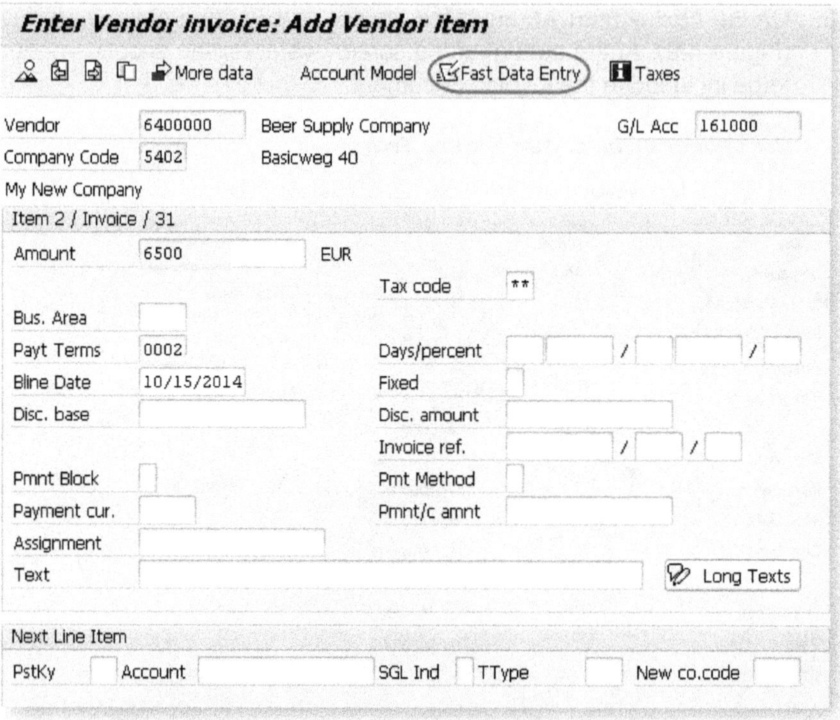

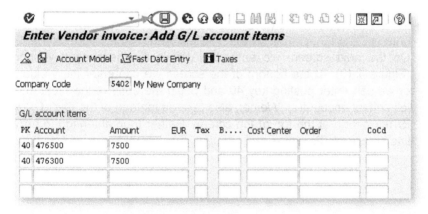

Figure 4.10: Posting a vendor invoice, F-43, step 4

5. Enter the line item details for the offsetting profit and loss accounts and click 🖫 to post the entry (Figure 4.11).

Figure 4.11: Posting a vendor invoice, F-43, step 5

6. If desired, use transaction FB03 (as described in Section 2.3.6) to display the document (Figure 4.12).

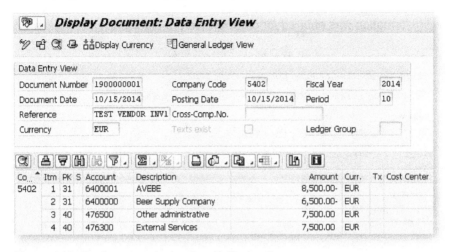

Figure 4.12: Posting a vendor invoice, F-43 step 6

4.3.2 FB65/F-41: Posting a credit memo

When we record a vendor credit memo received from our vendor, we create a debit entry to the vendor account and a credit entry (typically) to a profit and loss account. Similar to the situation for posting vendor invoices, the SAP system provides two transactions for posting credit memos to vendor accounts: FB65 and F-41.

Transaction FB65: Credit Memo

1. From the SAP Easy Access menu, navigate to: ACCOUNTING • FINANCIAL ACCOUNTING • ACCOUNTS PAYABLE • DOCUMENT ENTRY • FB65-CREDIT MEMO.

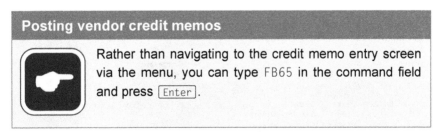

Posting vendor credit memos

Rather than navigating to the credit memo entry screen via the menu, you can type FB65 in the command field and press Enter.

2. Enter details for the document as shown in Figure 4.13 and then click 🖫. Press ⌈Enter⌉ to navigate past any warning messages related to posting periods, payment terms, or due dates. The fields in which information was entered for our example are highlighted.

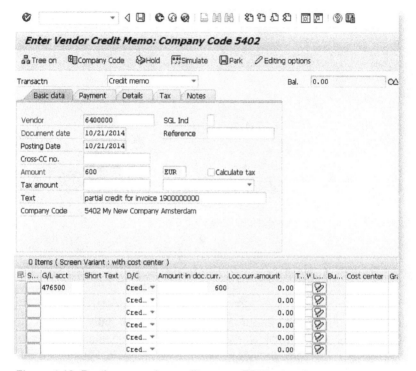

Figure 4.13: Posting a vendor credit memo, FB65, step 2

3. If desired, use transaction FB03 (as described in Section 2.3.6) to display the document (Figure 4.14).

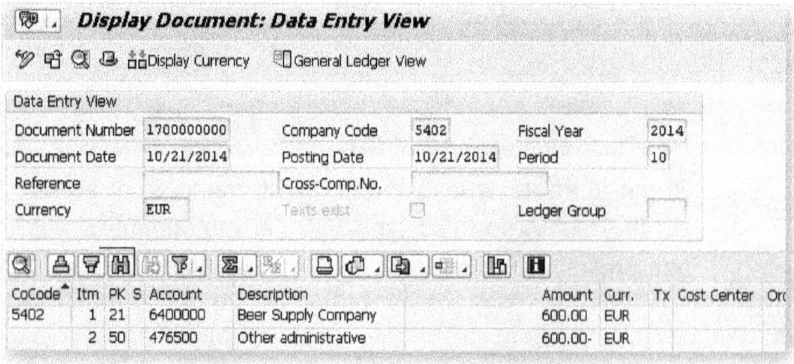

Figure 4.14: Posting a vendor credit memo, FB65, step 3

Transaction F-41: Credit Memo – General

1. From the SAP Easy Access menu, navigate to: ACCOUNTING • FINAN-CIAL ACCOUNTING • ACCOUNTS PAYABLE • DOCUMENT ENTRY • F-41 – CREDIT MEMO – GENERAL.

2. Enter the details for the document as shown in Figure 4.15 and then click ✅. Press [Enter] to navigate past any warning messages related to posting periods, payment terms, or due dates.

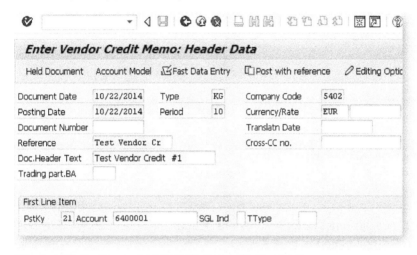

Figure 4.15: Posting a vendor credit memo, F-41, step 2

Posting keys

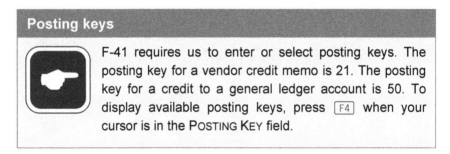

F-41 requires us to enter or select posting keys. The posting key for a vendor credit memo is 21. The posting key for a credit to a general ledger account is 50. To display available posting keys, press [F4] when your cursor is in the POSTING KEY field.

---

3. Enter the credit memo amount (Figure 4.16). At the bottom of the screen, enter the posting key and offsetting general ledger account for the credit memo. Press [Enter] to navigate past any warning messages related to posting periods, payment terms, or due dates.

147

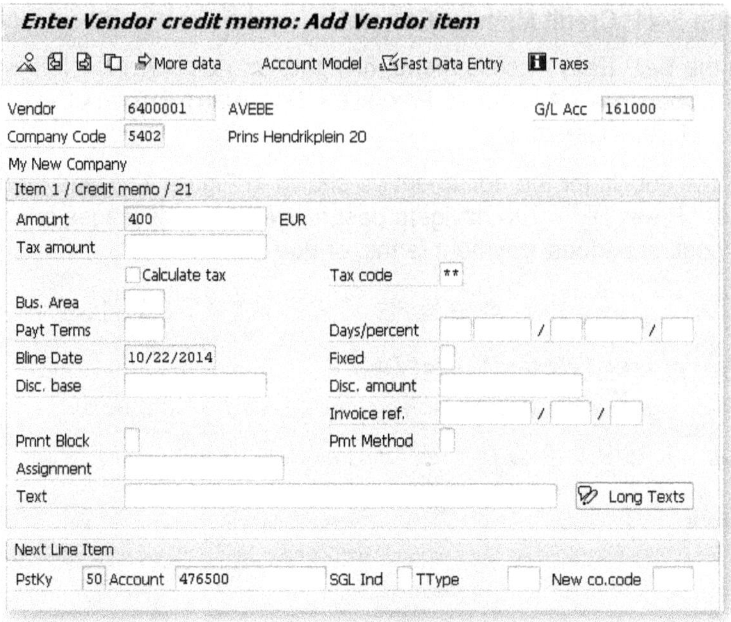

Figure 4.16: Posting a vendor credit memo, F-41, step 3

4. Enter the amount for the general ledger offset and click 💾 to post the credit memo (Figure 4.17).

Figure 4.17: Posting a vendor credit memo, F-41, step 4

5. Use FB03 (as described in Section 2.3.6) to display the document if desired (Figure 4.18):

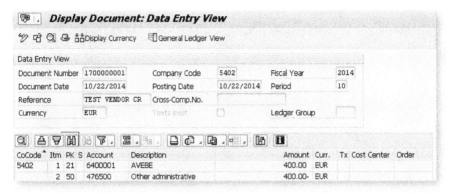

Figure 4.18: Posting a vendor credit memo, F-41, step 5

4.3.3 FV60/F-63/FV65/F-66: Parking vendor documents

Similar to parking for general ledger documents, which was detailed in Section 2.3.3, vendor documents can be entered and parked for subsequent posting. Just as we had several options for posting vendor invoices and credit memos, we have several options for parking accounts payable documents. After a document is parked, it can be posted with the same FBV0 transaction demonstrated for parked general ledger documents and illustrated in Figure 2.37 through Figure 2.41.

We will explore transaction FV60 Park or Edit Invoice in the steps below.

1. From the SAP Easy Access menu, navigate to: ACCOUNTING • FINANCIAL ACCOUNTING • ACCOUNTS PAYABLE • DOCUMENT ENTRY • DOCUMENT PARKING • FV60 – PARK OR EDIT INVOICE.

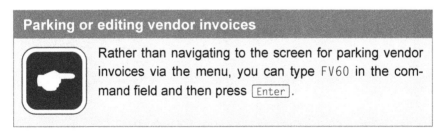

Parking or editing vendor invoices

Rather than navigating to the screen for parking vendor invoices via the menu, you can type FV60 in the command field and then press [Enter].

2. Enter details for the document and then choose 🖫 Save as completed (Figure 4.19).

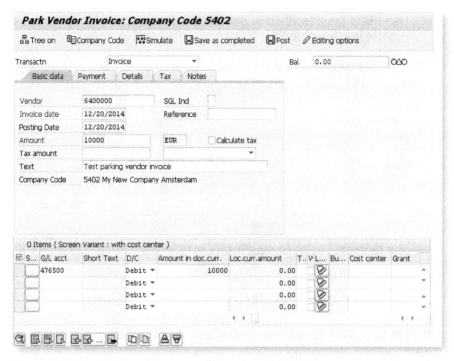

Figure 4.19: Parking or editing a vendor invoice, FV60, step 2

3. To post the invoice, follow the steps described in Section 2.3.3 FV50/FV50L: Parked documents. Use transaction FBV0 and enter the document number and press [Enter] or use the document list function to locate the document (Figure 4.20).

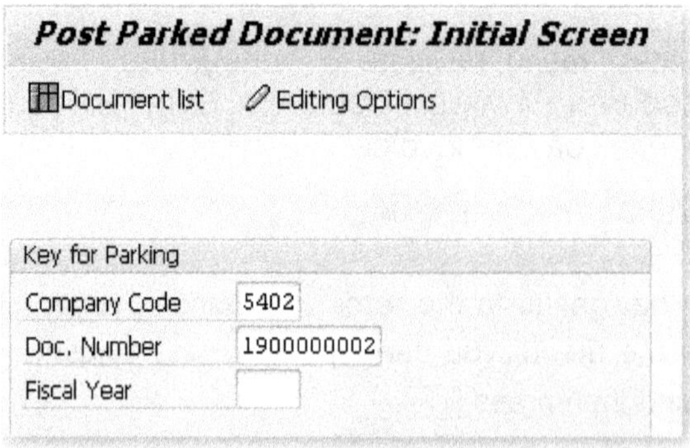

Post Parked Document: Initial Screen

Document list   Editing Options

Key for Parking	
Company Code	5402
Doc. Number	1900000002
Fiscal Year	

Figure 4.20: Parking or editing a vendor invoice, FV60, step 3

4. On the parked document editing screen, choose 🖫 Post (Figure 4.21).

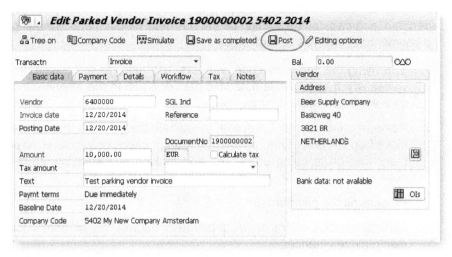

Figure 4.21: Parking or editing a vendor invoice, FV60, step 4

5. Use transaction FB03 (as described in Section 2.3.6) to display the document if desired (Figure 4.22).

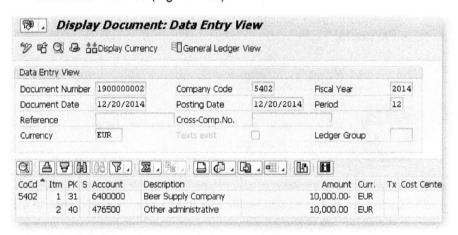

Figure 4.22: Parking or editing a vendor invoice, FV60, step 5

4.3.4. F110: Executing a payment run

An SAP payment run can create payments for several company codes, vendors, and invoices depending on the business requirements. Creating a payment run involves several steps:

1. Specifying the company code, vendors, and invoices to be paid. Invoices which have a due date less than or equal to the payment run date will be processed for payment.

2. Reviewing the payment proposal to validate the invoices that will be picked up for processing payments through check or whatever payment method is being processed and making any adjustments required.

3. Processing the payment run.

4. Printing checks or transmitting payment information to banks for electronic remittances.

For a sample payment run, we will perform all of the steps except printing the checks or transmitting payment information.

1. From the SAP Easy Access menu, navigate to: ACCOUNTING • FINANCIAL ACCOUNTING • ACCOUNTS PAYABLE • PERIODIC PROCESSING • F110 – PAYMENTS.

Creating payment runs

 Rather than navigating to the automatic payment transaction screen via the menu, you can type F110 in the command field and press [Enter].

---

2. Enter a run date and an identifier for the payment run and choose the PARAMETER tab (Figure 4.23).

3. Enter the parameters for creating the payment run and then choose the ADDITIONAL LOG tab (Figure 4.24).

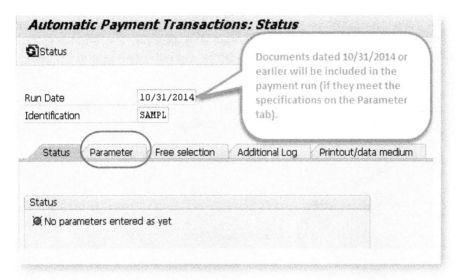

Figure 4.23: Creating a payment run, step 2

Figure 4.24: Creating a payment run, step 3

4. On the ADDITIONAL LOG tab (Figure 4.25) enter the desired criteria for an additional log to be generated and click 🖫. The additional logs can be helpful if there are any errors when the payment run is generated.

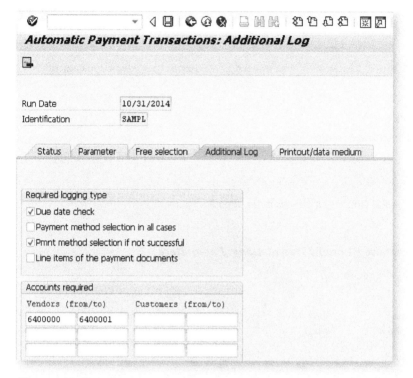

Figure 4.25: Creating a payment run, step 4

5. When the message ☑ Details have been saved for the run on 10/31/14 SAMPL appears, click 🕐 in the toolbar at the top of the screen to return to the initial screen.

6. In Figure 4.26, note the change in status; parameters have been entered. Select the PROPOSAL icon. Press Enter to navigate past any warning messages regarding the payment run occurring in the past.

Figure 4.26: Creating a payment run, step 6

7. Enter a start date or, as in our example, choose to start the proposal immediately (Figure 4.27). Click ✔ to continue.

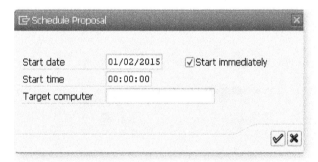

Figure 4.27: Creating a payment run, step 7

8. In Figure 4.28, note that the status has changed to indicate a proposal is running. Click the REFRESH STATUS icon several times until the status changes to indicate that the payment proposal is complete.

Figure 4.28: Creating a payment run, step 8

9. When the status reflects that a payment proposal has been created, choose $\square$ Proposal to see messages related to the payment run (Figure 4.29).

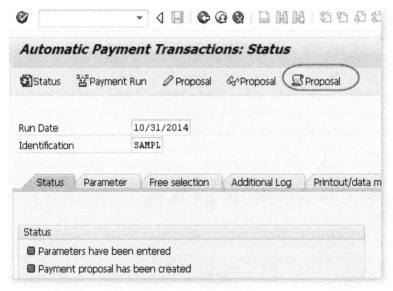

Figure 4.29: Creating a payment run, step 9

10. After reviewing the log (Figure 4.30), click 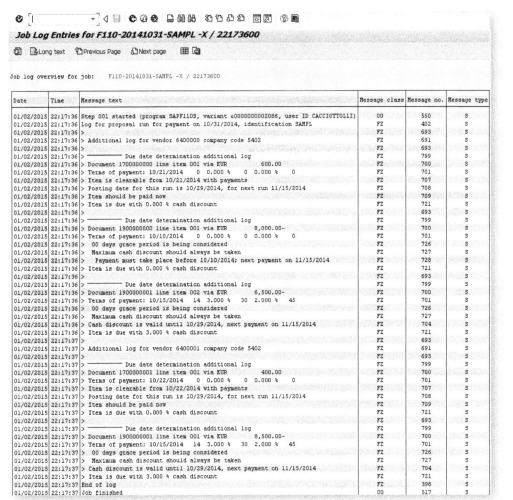 and then choose ✐ Proposal to make changes to the items that are proposed for inclusion in our payment run.

Figure 4.30: Creating a payment run, step 10

11. You can choose to edit documents for a specific accounting clerk or all accounting clerks (Figure 4.31). Click ✅ to continue.

Figure 4.31: Creating a payment run, step 11

12. The total payments to be made to each vendor that are included in the proposal are shown in Figure 4.32. After selecting a vendor line, select CHOOSE.

Figure 4.32: Creating a payment run, step 12

13. In Figure 4.33, we can see that the payments to vendor 6400000 include a deduction for the credit memo of EUR 600.00. Let's change our payment to exclude this deduction. Select the item then choose CHANGE.

14. Select PAYMENT BLOCK A, click ✓ (Figure 4.34), and then choose ⟳ from the toolbar.

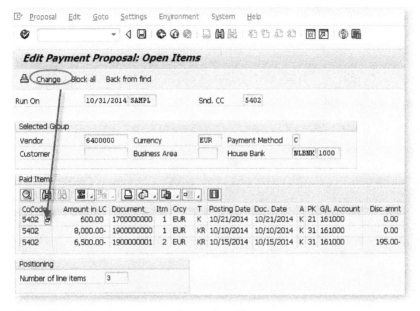

Figure 4.33: Creating a payment run, step 13

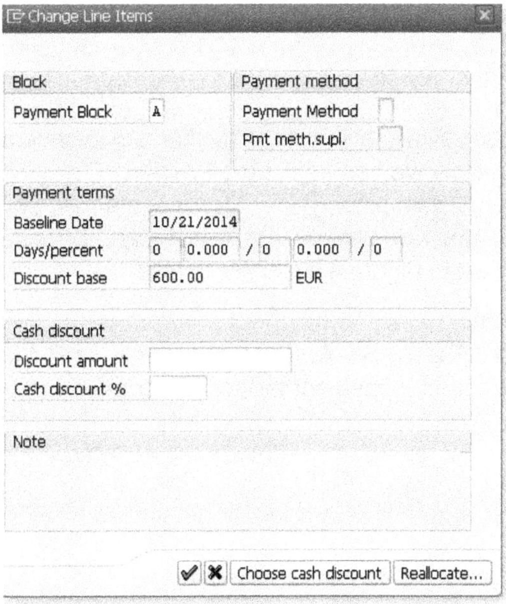

Figure 4.34: Creating a payment run, step 14

15. In Figure 4.35, note that the credit memo is now de-selected and the outgoing payment amount has increased by EUR 600.00. Click and then select [Yes] when prompted to save changes.

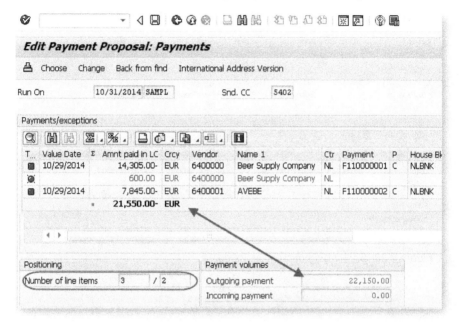

Figure 4.35: Creating a payment run, step 15

16. We can see from the STATUS tab in Figure 4.36 that our payment proposal has been edited. Now we can select the PAYMENT RUN icon to process the payment run. Again press [Enter] to navigate past any warning messages about the run date being in the past. Choose START IMMEDIATELY as shown in Figure 4.27.

17. A message appears indicating that the payment program is running (Figure 4.37). Click the (REFRESH) STATUS icon repeatedly until the status changes to indicate that the payment proposal is complete.

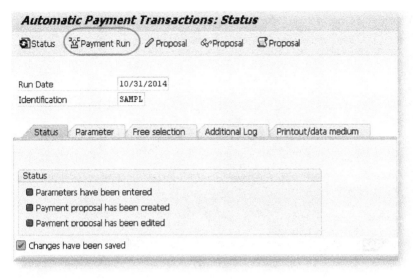

Figure 4.36: Creating a payment run, step 16

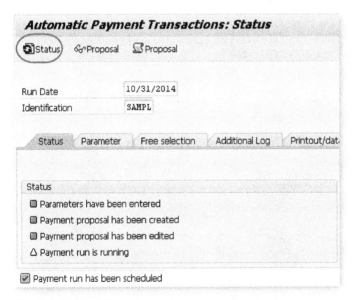

Figure 4.37: Creating a payment run, step 17

18. After the payment run is completed, note the message that payment postings have been executed (Figure 4.38).

Figure 4.38: Creating a payment run, step 18

19. If desired, use transaction FB03 (as described in Section 2.3.6) to display the documents (Figure 4.39).

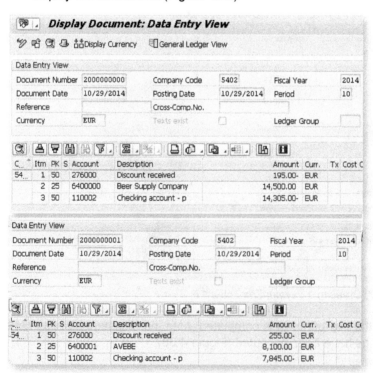

Figure 4.39: Creating a payment run, step 19

4.3.5 F-53: Posting payments

We have seen how we can set up a payment run for groups of vendors and invoices. You can use transaction F-53 to process a single manual payment.

In the following example, we will record a payment for invoice 1900000002 to vendor 6400000.

1. From the SAP Easy Access menu, navigate to: ACCOUNTING • FINAN-CIAL ACCOUNTING • ACCOUNTS PAYABLE • DOCUMENT ENTRY • OUT-GOING PAYMENT • F-53 – POST.

2. Enter details for the payment (Figure 4.40). Since we know the number of the document that will be paid, the additional selections include a document number. Choose PROCESS OPEN ITEMS.

Post Outgoing Payments: Header Data

Process Open Items

Document Date	12/28/2014	Type	KZ	Company Code	5402
Posting Date	12/28/2014	Period	12	Currency/Rate	EUR
Document Number				Translatn Date	
Reference				Cross-CC no.	
Doc.Header Text	test payment			Trading part.BA	
Clearing text	manual payment				

Bank Data

Account	110002	Business Area	
Amount	10000	Amount in LC	
Bank charges		LC bank charges	
Value date	12/28/2014	Profit Center	
Text		Assignment	

Open Item Selection			Additional Selections	
Account	6400000		○ None	
Account Type	K	☐ Other accounts	○ Amount	
Special G/L ind		☑ Standard OIs	⦿ Document Number	
Pmnt advice no.			○ Posting Date	
☐ Distribute by age			○ Dunning Area	
☐ Automatic search			○ Others	

Figure 4.40: Posting a payment, F-53, step 2

3. Enter the document number and choose PROCESS OPEN ITEMS (Figure 4.41).

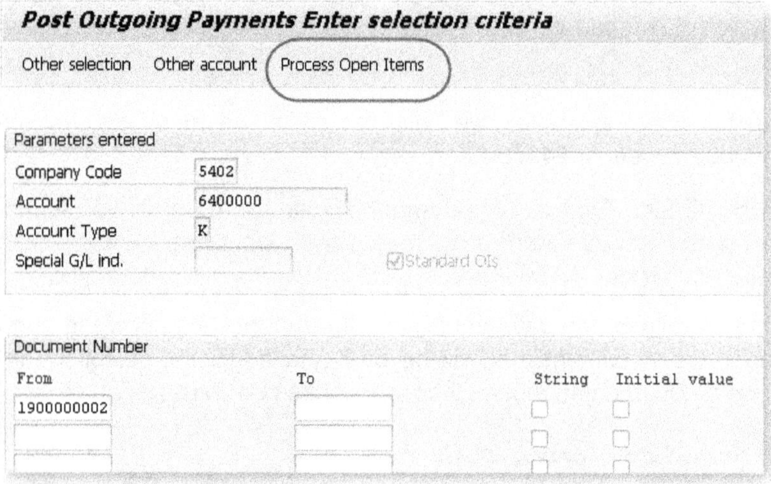

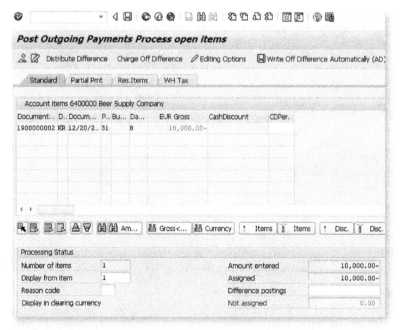

Figure 4.41: Posting a payment, F-53, step 3

4. With the amount assigned to documents being equal to the payment amount, click 🖫 to post the payment (Figure 4.42).

Figure 4.42: Posting a payment, F-53, step 4

5. If desired, use transaction FB03 (as described in Section 2.3.6) to display the documents (Figure 4.43).

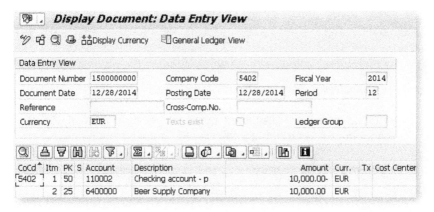

Figure 4.43: Posting a payment, F-53, step 5

4.4 SAP Accounts Payable (AP) reports

We will now take a look at just a few of the common reports available. Once you have explored these examples, you should be able to navigate through the SAP AP Information System to gather any information required regarding accounts payable.

4.4.1 Displaying vendor balances

1. To display the vendor balances, from the SAP Easy Access menu, navigate to: ACCOUNTING • FINANCIAL ACCOUNTING • ACCOUNTS PAYA-BLE • ACCOUNT • FK10N – DISPLAY BALANCES.

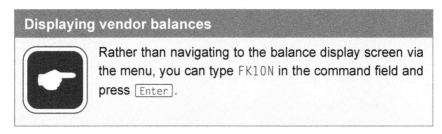

Displaying vendor balances

Rather than navigating to the balance display screen via the menu, you can type FK10N in the command field and press Enter.

2. Enter a vendor number, company code, and fiscal year and then click to execute the report (Figure 4.44).

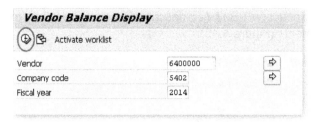

Figure 4.44: Displaying vendor balances, step 2

3. Vendor balances are displayed by fiscal period (Figure 4.45). You can double-click an amount to display the detailed line items.

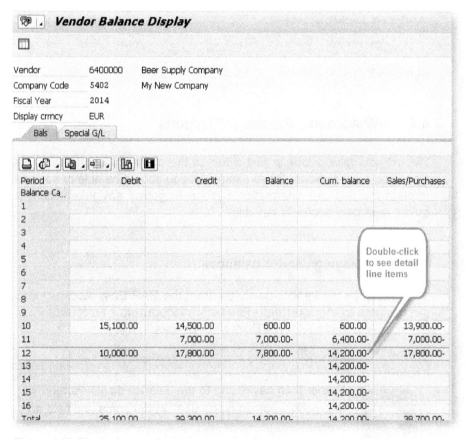

Figure 4.45: Displaying vendor balances, step 3

4. The line items that make up the balance are displayed (Figure 4.46).

Vendor Line Item Display

Vendor   6400000
Company Code   5402

Name   Beer Supply Company
City

St	DocumentNo	Type	Doc. Date	Amount in local cur.	LCurr	Clrng doc.	T
	1700000000	KG	10/21/2014	600.00	EUR		P
	1900000005	KR	11/17/2014	3,000.00-	EUR		
	1900000006	KR	11/18/2014	4,000.00-	EUR		
	1900000007	KR	12/10/2014	6,200.00-	EUR		
	1900000008	KR	12/12/2014	1,600.00-	EUR		
*				14,200.00-	EUR		
	1500000000	KZ	12/28/2014	10,000.00	EUR	1500000000	m
	1900000002	KR	12/20/2014	10,000.00-	EUR	1500000000	T
	1900000000	KR	10/10/2014	8,000.00-	EUR	2000000000	
	1900000001	KR	10/15/2014	6,500.00-	EUR	2000000000	
	2000000000	ZP	10/29/2014	14,500.00	EUR	2000000000	
*				0.00	EUR		
** Account 6400000				14,200.00-	EUR		

Figure 4.46: Displaying vendor balances, step 4

4.4.2   Displaying vendor line items

Rather than navigating to the line items from the vendor balance display, you can use the line item display transaction.

1.   From the SAP Easy Access menu, navigate to: ACCOUNTING • FINAN-
     CIAL ACCOUNTING • ACCOUNTS PAYABLE • ACCOUNT • FBL1N – DIS-
     PLAY/CHANGE LINE ITEMS.

Displaying vendor line items

 Rather than navigating to the screen for displaying vendor line items via the menu, you can type FBL1N in the
command field and press [Enter].

---

2. Enter a vendor account number and company code. Choose the type of line items to be displayed. In Figure 4.47, we are choosing to display all of the line items posted for vendor 6400001.

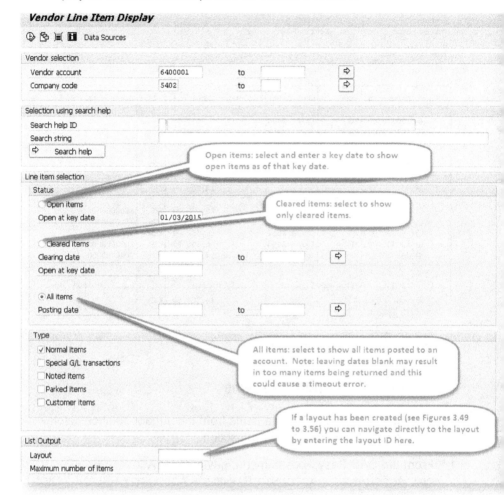

Figure 4.47: Displaying vendor line items, step 2

3. Vendor line items are displayed (Figure 4.48).

4. To display details, double-click a line item. In Figure 4.49, note that for the document selected, we can see details including the clearing document—the ZP payment document that was recorded with our payment run demonstrated in Section 4.3.4.

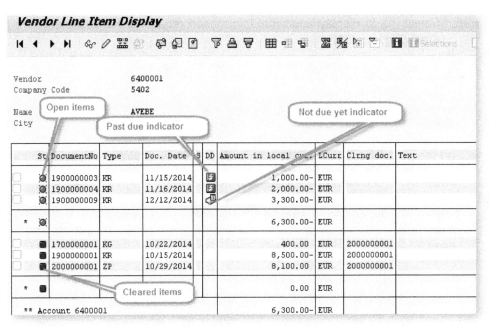

Vendor Line Item Display

Vendor 6400001
Company Code 5402

Name AVEBE
City

Open items

Past due indicator

Not due yet indicator

St	DocumentNo	Type	Doc. Date	S	DD	Amount in local cu...	LCurr	Clrng doc.	Text
☒	1900000003	KR	11/15/2014		🖪	1,000.00-	EUR		
☒	1900000004	KR	11/16/2014		🖪	2,000.00-	EUR		
☒	1900000009	KR	12/12/2014		🖪	3,300.00-	EUR		
* ☒						6,300.00-	EUR		
■	1700000001	KG	10/22/2014			400.00	EUR	2000000001	
■	1900000001	KR	10/15/2014			8,500.00	EUR	2000000001	
■	2000000001	ZP	10/29/2014			8,100.00	EUR	2000000001	
* ■						0.00	EUR		
**	Account 6400001					6,300.00-	EUR		

Cleared items

Figure 4.48: Displaying vendor line items, step 3

Display Document: Line Item 001

Additional Data

Vendor 6400001 AVEBE G/L Acc 161000
Company Code 5402 Prins Hendrikplein 20
My New Company Doc. no. 1900000001

Line Item 1 / Invoice / 31

Amount 8,500.00 EUR
Tax code

Additional Data

Bus. Area
Disc. base 8,500.00 EUR Disc. amount 255.00 EUR
Payt Terms 0002 Days/percent 14 3.000 % 30 2.000 % 45
Bline Date 10/15/2014 Fixed
Pmnt Block Invoice Ref. / / 0
Payment cur. Pmnt/c amnt 0.00
Pmt Method
Clearing 10/29/2014 / 2000000001
Assignment
Text Long text

Figure 4.49: Displaying vendor line items, step 4

5. Select ![icon] to display additional information regarding the document entry (Figure 4.50).

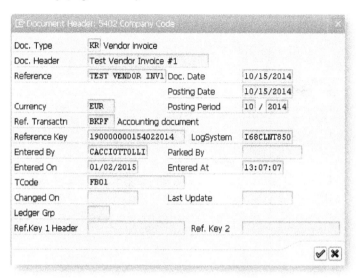

Figure 4.50: Displaying vendor line items, step 5

6. Select ![icon] (see Figure 4.49) to display the document entry view as we saw with transaction FB03 (Figure 4.51).

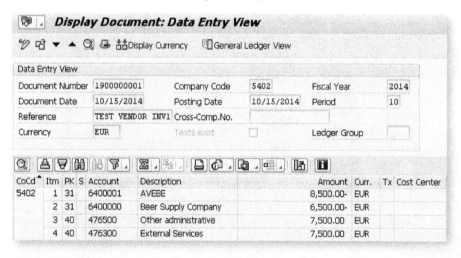

Figure 4.51: Displaying vendor line items, step 6

4.4.3 Accessing the SAP AP Information System

In this section, we will explore just one of the AP reports delivered with SAP, but you are encouraged to use the techniques learned here and in the AR Information System to view the many reports available.

To access the reports, from the SAP Easy Access menu, navigate to the Accounts Payable Information System (Figure 4.52).

ACCOUNTING • FINANCIAL ACCOUNTING • ACCOUNTS PAYABLE • INFORMATION SYSTEM • REPORTS FOR ACCOUNTS PAYABLE ACCOUNTING

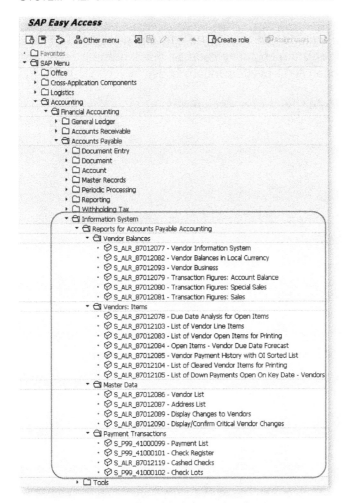

Figure 4.52: Accounts Payable Information System

Due date analysis for open items

1. Select report S_ALR_87012078 from the Information System by double-clicking it.

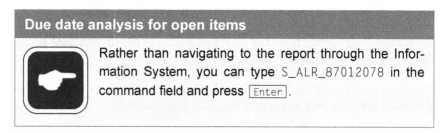

Due date analysis for open items

Rather than navigating to the report through the Information System, you can type S_ALR_87012078 in the command field and press ⌈Enter⌉.

2. Enter selection criteria and click ⊕ to execute the report. In Figure 4.53 we enter only the company code so that the report returns all vendors with open items in the company code.

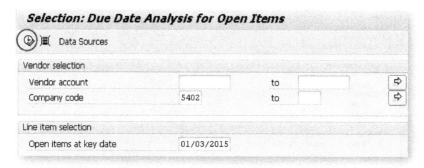

Figure 4.53: Due date analysis for open items report, step 2

3. Once the report has been executed (Figure 4.54), details by vendor appear in the top section of the report and a summary of open items appears below.

4. Double-click DOCUMENT TYPE in the navigation panel on the left and note that the report is now broken down by document type (Figure 4.55).

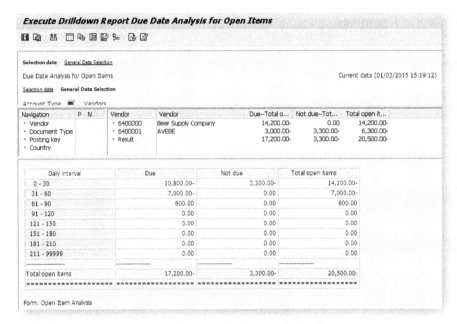

Figure 4.54: Due date analysis for open items report, step 3

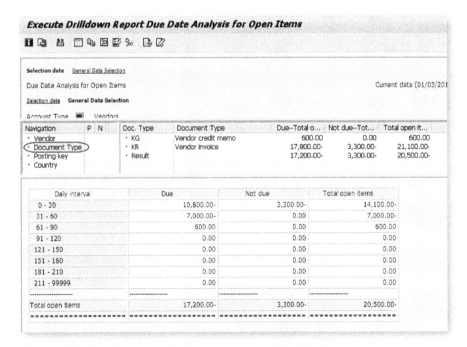

Figure 4.55: Due date analysis for open items report, step 4

4.5 Exercises

4.5.1 Create a vendor

Account group	0066 – New Vendors (similar to group 0004)
Vendor info	Hoogeveen Prins Hendrikstraat 24 7902 BZ Hoogeveen Netherlands
Reconciliation account	161000

4.5.2 Post a vendor invoice

Vendor	Deventer
Invoice #1 info Date Reference Amount GL offset	 Today's date New invoice 1 EUR 7000 476500

4.5.3 Display line items for the vendor

5 Configuration for getting started with SAP FI

This chapter provides an explanation of the basic configuration needed in order to perform the exercises contained in this book.

Step-by-step instructions are not given; instead, the menu paths and/or transaction codes for the basic configuration are given along with the values used in creating the exercises.

Unless otherwise indicated, all of the menu paths listed start from the Customizing menu, which can be accessed by executing transaction SPRO.

5.1   Create a Company Code

5.1.1   Copy company code

ENTERPRISE STRUCTURE • DEFINITION • FINANCIAL ACCOUNTING • EDIT, COPY, DELETE, CHECK COMPANY CODE (transaction OX02)

Company Code	5402
Name	My Company Code
City	Amsterdam
Country	NL
Currency	EUR
Street/House	Surinmestratt 27
Postal Code	2585 GJ
City	Den Haug
Country	NL
PO Box	90922
Postal Code	2595 GJ

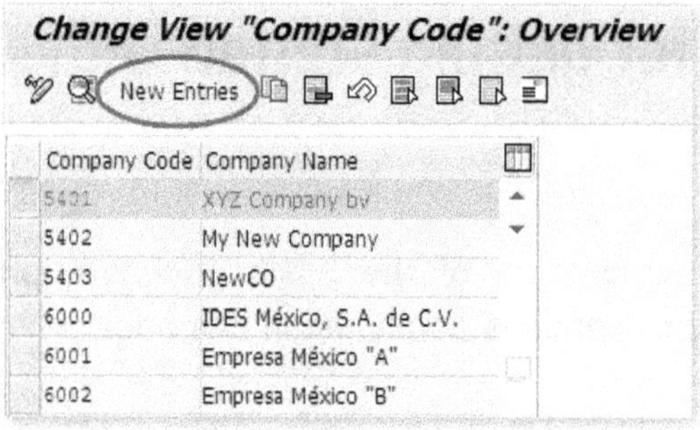

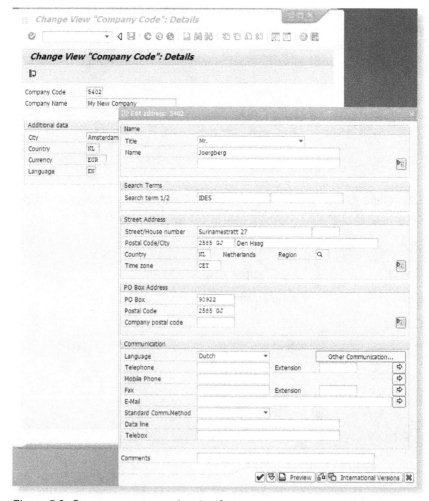

Figure 5.1: Copy a company code, step 1

Figure 5.2: Copy a company code, step 2

5.1.2   Assign global parameters

FINANCIAL ACCOUNTING (NEW) • FINANCIAL ACCOUNTING GLOBAL SETTINGS (NEW) • GLOBAL PARAMETERS FOR COMPANY CODE • ENTER GLOBAL PARAMETERS (transaction OBY6)

Figure 5.3: Global parameters for sample company code

5.2   Assign company code to controlling area

CONTROLLING • GENERAL CONTROLLING • ORGANIZATION • MAINTAIN CONTROLLING AREA (transaction OKKP)

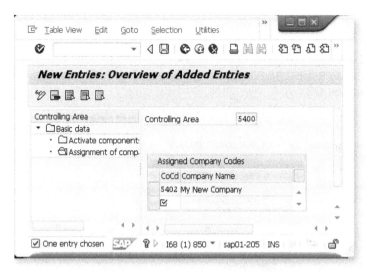

Figure 5.4: Assign a company code to controlling area 5400

5.3 Copy chart of accounts to company code

In Section 5.1.2 we assigned the chart of accounts INT1 to our company code; however, the actual accounts in the chart of accounts need to be extended to the company code. There is an SAP transaction that enables all of the accounts used in one company code to be extended to another company code:

ACCOUNTING • FINANCIAL ACCOUNTING • GENERAL LEDGER • MASTER REC-ORDS • G/L ACCOUNTS • COMPARE COMPANY CODE • FS15 – SEND (transaction FS15)

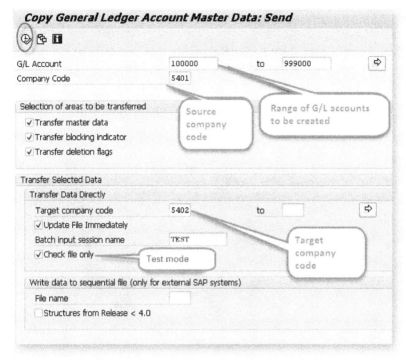

Figure 5.5: Copy chart of accounts to company code

5.4 Prepare for General Ledger document entry

5.4.1 Deactivate document splitting for company code

FINANCIAL ACCOUNTING (NEW) • GENERAL LEDGER ACCOUNTING (NEW) • BUSINESS TRANSACTIONS • DOCUMENT SPLITTING • ACTIVATE DOCUMENT SPLITTING

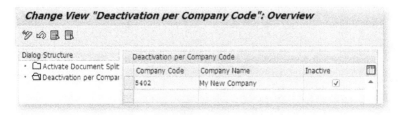

Figure 5.6: Deactivate document splitting

5.4.2 Assign number ranges to documents

FINANCIAL ACCOUNTING (NEW) • FINANCIAL ACCOUNTING GLOBAL SETTINGS (NEW) • DOCUMENT • DOCUMENT NUMBER RANGES • DOCUMENTS IN ENTRY VIEW • COPY TO COMPANY CODE (transaction OBH1)

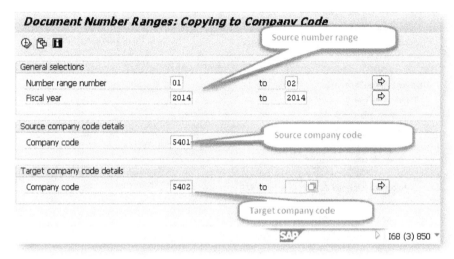

Figure 5.7: Copy document number ranges to company code

5.4.3 Create number range for recurring documents

FINANCIAL ACCOUNTING (NEW) • FINANCIAL ACCOUNTING GLOBAL SETTINGS (NEW) • DOCUMENT • DOCUMENT NUMBER RANGES • DOCUMENTS IN ENTRY VIEW • DEFINE DOCUMENT NUMBER RANGES FOR ENTRY VIEW (transaction FBN1)

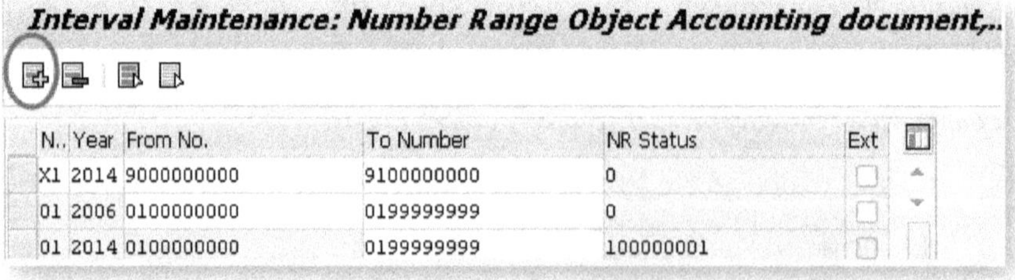

Interval Maintenance: Number Range Object Accounting document,..

N..	Year	From No.	To Number	NR Status	Ext	
X1	2014	9000000000	9100000000	0	☐	▲
01	2006	0100000000	0199999999	0	☐	▼
01	2014	0100000000	0199999999	100000001	☐	

Figure 5.8: Create number ranges for recurring documents

5.4.4 Define tolerance groups

FINANCIAL ACCOUNTING (NEW) • GENERAL LEDGER ACCOUNTING (NEW) • BUSINESS TRANSACTIONS • OPEN ITEM CLEARING • OPEN ITEM PROCESSING • CLEARING DIFFERENCES • DEFINE TOLERANCE GROUPS FOR EMPLOYEES (transaction OBA4)

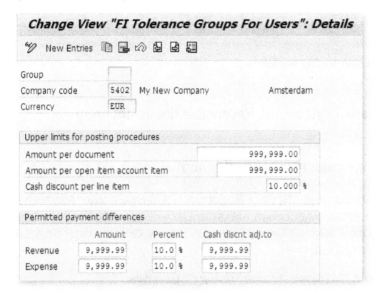

Figure 5.9: Define tolerance groups

GROUP can be left blank if all users will have the same tolerance levels.

5.4.5 Open posting periods

FINANCIAL ACCOUNTING (NEW) • FINANCIAL ACCOUNTING GLOBAL SETTINGS (NEW) • FISCAL YEAR AND POSTING PERIODS • POSTING PERIODS • OPEN AND CLOSE POSTING PERIODS

Change View "Posting Periods: Specify Time Intervals": Overview

New Entries 🗋 🗐 🖎 🗐 🖳 🗟

Var.	A	From acct	To account	From per.1	Year	To period	Year	From per.2	Year	To period	Year	AuGr
1000	+		1	2014	12		2015	1	2014	12	2015	
1000	A		ZZZZZZZZZZ	1	2014	12		2015	1	2014	12	2015
1000	D		ZZZZZZZZZZ	1	2014	12		2015	1	2014	12	2015
1000	K		ZZZZZZZZZZ	1	2014	12		2015	1	2014	12	2015
1000	M		ZZZZZZZZZZ	1	2014	12		2015	1	2014	12	2015
1000	S		ZZZZZZZZZZ	1	2014	12		2015	1	2014	12	2015

Figure 5.10: Open posting periods

5.5   Prepare for Accounts Receivable document entry

5.5.1   Create customer account group

FINANCIAL ACCOUNTING (NEW) • ACCOUNTS RECEIVABLE AND ACCOUNTS PAYABLE • CUSTOMER ACCOUNTS • MASTER DATA • PREPARATIONS FOR CREATING CUSTOMER MASTER DATA • DEFINE ACCOUNT GROUPS WITH SCREEN LAYOUT (CUSTOMERS)

Change View "Customer Account Groups": Overview

New entries 🗐 🗑 🖳 🖳 🗟

Group	Name
0003	Payer
0004	Bill-to party
0005	Prospective customer
0006	Competitor
0007	Sales partner
0012	Hierarchy node

Change View "Customer Account Groups": Details of Selected Set

Expand Field Status

Account group   0088

General data
Meaning   Standard Customer
One-time account   ☐
Output determ.proc.   ☐

Field status
General data
Company code data
Sales data

Figure 5.11: Create a customer account group

182

5.5.2 Create customer number ranges

FINANCIAL ACCOUNTING (NEW) • ACCOUNTS RECEIVABLE AND ACCOUNTS PAYABLE • CUSTOMER ACCOUNTS • MASTER DATA • PREPARATIONS FOR CREATING CUSTOMER MASTER DATA • CREATE NUMBER RANGES FOR CUSTOMER ACCOUNTS (transaction XDN1)

Maintain Intervals: Customer

Leave blank for internally assigned numbers.

N.	From No.	To Number	NR Status	Ext
54	0050000000	0059999999	0	☐
01	0000000001	0000099999	0	☑
02	0000100000	0000199999	100190	☐
03	1000000000	1000099999	1000000039	☐
04	0000200000	0000299999	0	☑

Figure 5.12: Create customer number ranges

5.5.3 Assign number range to customer group

FINANCIAL ACCOUNTING (NEW) • ACCOUNTS RECEIVABLE AND ACCOUNTS PAYABLE • CUSTOMER ACCOUNTS • MASTER DATA • PREPARATIONS FOR CREATING CUSTOMER MASTER DATA • ASSIGN NUMBER RANGES TO CUSTOMER ACCOUNT GROUPS

Change View "Assign Customer Acct Groups->Number

Group	Name	Number range
0170	Consumer	08
088	Standard Customer	54
1111	Sold-to party - 0001	10
3500	Sold-to party - FI-CAX	02
BR01	National Brazilian Customer	XX
BR02	Internacional brazilian Custom	XX
CPB1	Sold-to party (Beverage)	XX

Figure 5.13: Assign number range to customer group

5.5.4 Maintain payment terms

FINANCIAL ACCOUNTING (NEW) • ACCOUNTS RECEIVABLE AND ACCOUNTS PAYABLE • BUSINESS TRANSACTIONS • OUTGOING INVOICES/CREDIT MEMOS • MAINTAIN TERMS OF PAYMENT

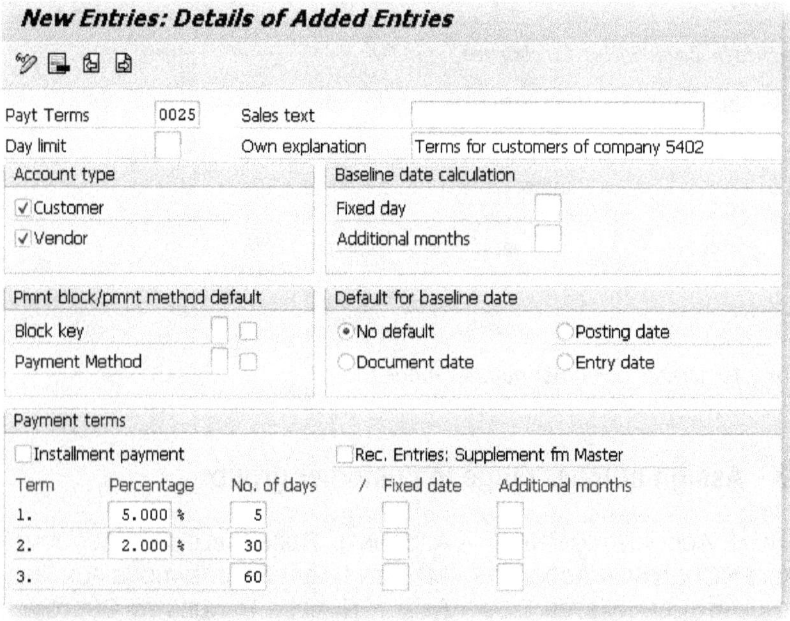

Figure 5.14: Maintain payment terms

5.5.5 Define reason codes

FINANCIAL ACCOUNTING (NEW) • ACCOUNTS RECEIVABLE AND ACCOUNTS PAYABLE • BUSINESS TRANSACTIONS • INCOMING PAYMENTS • INCOMING PAYMENTS GLOBAL SETTINGS • OVERPAYMENT/UNDERPAYMENT • DEFINE REASON CODES (transaction OBBE)

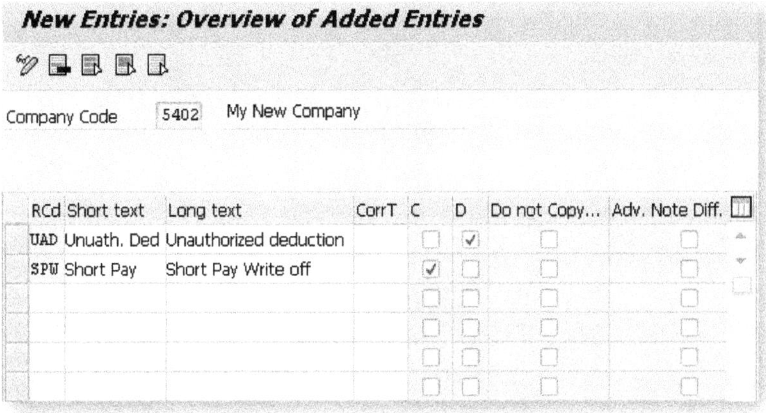

New Entries: Overview of Added Entries

Company Code 5402 My New Company

RCd	Short text	Long text	CorrT	C	D	Do not Copy...	Adv. Note Diff.
UAD	Unuath. Ded	Unauthorized deduction			✓		
SPW	Short Pay	Short Pay Write off		✓			

Figure 5.15: Define reason codes

5.5.6 Default account assignments

FINANCIAL ACCOUNTING (NEW) • ACCOUNTS RECEIVABLE AND ACCOUNTS PAYABLE • BUSINESS TRANSACTIONS • INCOMING PAYMENTS • INCOMING PAYMENTS GLOBAL SETTINGS • DEFINE ACCOUNTS FOR CASH DISCOUNT GRANTED (transaction OBXI)

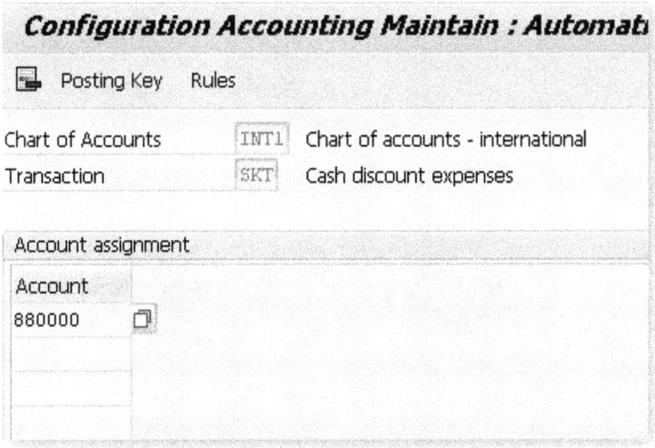

Configuration Accounting Maintain : Automati

Posting Key Rules

Chart of Accounts   INT1   Chart of accounts - international
Transaction   SKT   Cash discount expenses

Account assignment

Account
880000

Figure 5.16: Default account assignment for customer discounts

FINANCIAL ACCOUNTING (NEW) • ACCOUNTS RECEIVABLE AND ACCOUNTS PAYABLE • BUSINESS TRANSACTIONS • INCOMING PAYMENTS • INCOMING PAYMENTS GLOBAL SETTINGS • DEFINE ACCOUNTS FOR OVERPAYMENTS/UNDERPAYMENTS (transaction OBXL)

185

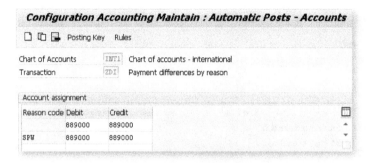

Figure 5.17: Default account assignment for overpayments/underpayments by reason code

5.5.7 Define document number ranges for customer invoices

FINANCIAL ACCOUNTING (NEW) • FINANCIAL ACCOUNTING GLOBAL SETTINGS (NEW) • DOCUMENT • DOCUMENT TYPES • DEFINE DOCUMENT TYPES FOR ENTRY VIEW (transaction OBA7)

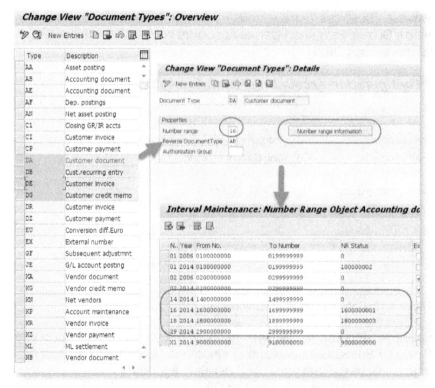

Figure 5.18: Define number ranges for customer invoices

5.6   Prepare for Accounts Payable document entry

5.6.1   Create house bank

FINANCIAL ACCOUNTING (NEW) • BANK ACCOUNTING • BANK ACCOUNTS • DEFINE HOUSE BANKS (transaction FI12)

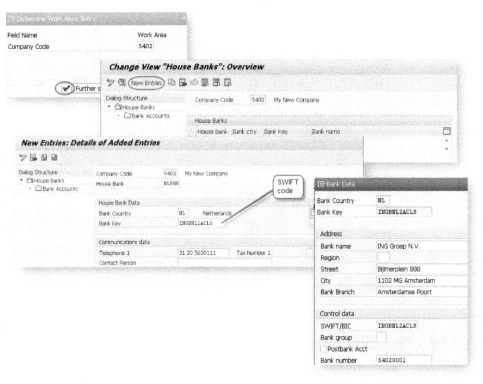

Figure 5.19: Create the house bank

5.6.2   Set up company codes for payment transactions

FINANCIAL ACCOUNTING (NEW) • ACCOUNTS RECEIVABLE AND ACCOUNTS PAYABLE • BUSINESS TRANSACTIONS • OUTGOING PAYMENTS • AUTOMATIC OUTGOING PAYMENTS • PAYMENT METHOD/BANK SELECTION FOR PAYMENT PROGRAM • SET UP ALL COMPANY CODES FOR PAYMENT TRANSACTIONS

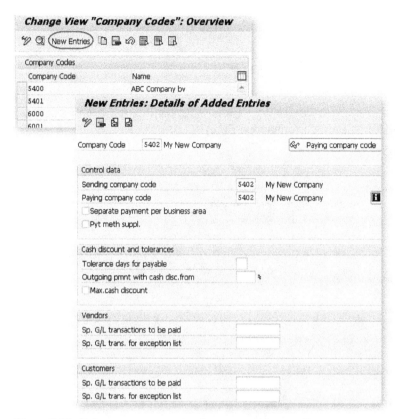

Figure 5.20: Set up company codes for payment transactions

5.6.3 Set up paying company code for payment transactions

FINANCIAL ACCOUNTING (NEW) • ACCOUNTS RECEIVABLE AND ACCOUNTS PAYABLE • BUSINESS TRANSACTIONS • OUTGOING PAYMENTS • AUTOMATIC OUTGOING PAYMENTS • PAYMENT METHOD/BANK SELECTION FOR PAYMENT PROGRAM • SET UP PAYING COMPANY CODES FOR PAYMENT TRANSACTIONS

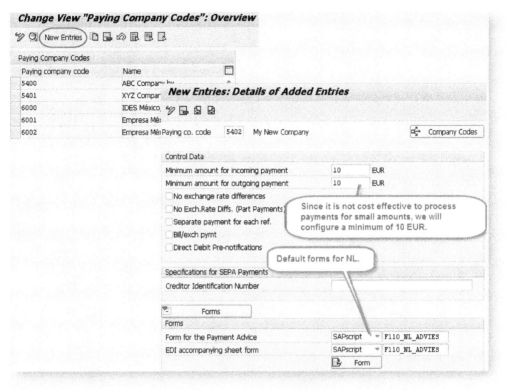

Figure 5.21: Set up paying company code for payment transactions

5.6.4 Set up payment methods per country

FINANCIAL ACCOUNTING (NEW) • ACCOUNTS RECEIVABLE AND ACCOUNTS PAYABLE • BUSINESS TRANSACTIONS • OUTGOING PAYMENTS • AUTOMATIC OUTGOING PAYMENTS • PAYMENT METHOD/BANK SELECTION FOR PAYMENT PROGRAM • SET UP PAYMENT METHODS PER COUNTRY FOR PAYMENT TRANSACTIONS

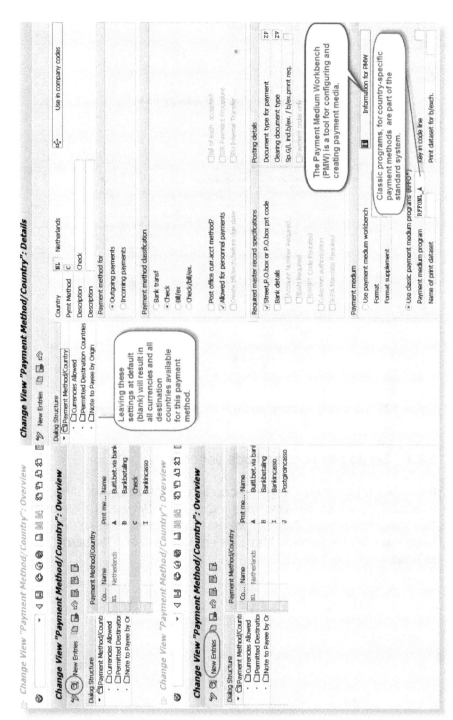

Figure 5.22: Set up payment methods per country

5.6.5 Set up payment method per company code

FINANCIAL ACCOUNTING (NEW) • ACCOUNTS RECEIVABLE AND ACCOUNTS PAYABLE • BUSINESS TRANSACTIONS • OUTGOING PAYMENTS • AUTOMATIC OUTGOING PAYMENTS • PAYMENT METHOD/BANK SELECTION FOR PAYMENT PROGRAM • SET UP PAYMENT METHODS PER COMPANY CODE FOR PAYMENT TRANSACTIONS

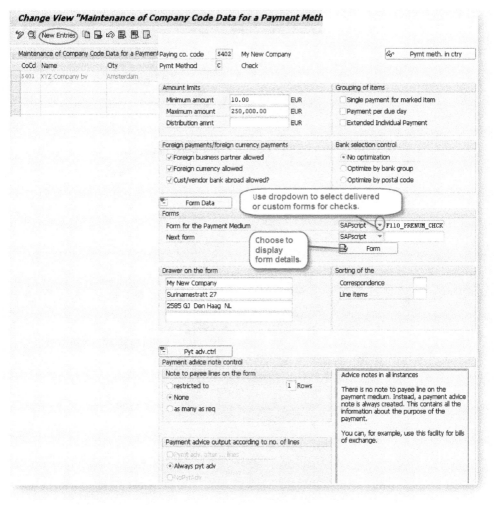

Figure 5.23: Set up a payment method per company code

5.6.6 Set up bank determination for payment transactions

FINANCIAL ACCOUNTING (NEW) • ACCOUNTS RECEIVABLE AND ACCOUNTS PAYABLE • BUSINESS TRANSACTIONS • OUTGOING PAYMENTS • AUTOMATIC OUTGOING PAYMENTS • PAYMENT METHOD/BANK SELECTION FOR PAYMENT PROGRAM • SET UP BANK DETERMINATION FOR PAYMENT TRANSACTIONS

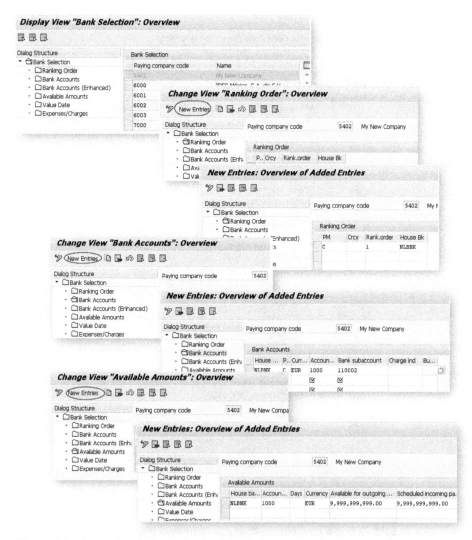

Figure 5.24: Set up bank determination for payment transactions

5.6.7 Create number ranges for vendors

FINANCIAL ACCOUNTING (NEW) • ACCOUNTS RECEIVABLE AND ACCOUNTS PAYABLE • VENDOR ACCOUNTS • MASTER DATA • PREPARATIONS FOR CREATING VENDOR MASTER DATA • CREATE NUMBER RANGES FOR VENDOR ACCOUNTS (transaction XKN1)

N..	From No.	To Number	NR Status	Ext
64	0006400000	0006999999	0	☐
01	0000000001	0000099999	0	☑
02	0000100000	0000199999	100237	☐
03	0000200000	0000299999	200059	☐
04	0000300000	0000399999	0	☑

Maintain Intervals: Vendor

Leave blank for internally assigned numbers.

Figure 5.25: Create number ranges for vendors

5.6.8 Define vendor account groups

FINANCIAL ACCOUNTING (NEW) • ACCOUNTS RECEIVABLE AND ACCOUNTS PAYABLE • VENDOR ACCOUNTS • MASTER DATA • PREPARATIONS FOR CREATING VENDOR MASTER DATA • DEFINE ACCOUNT GROUPS WITH SCREEN LAYOUT (VENDORS)

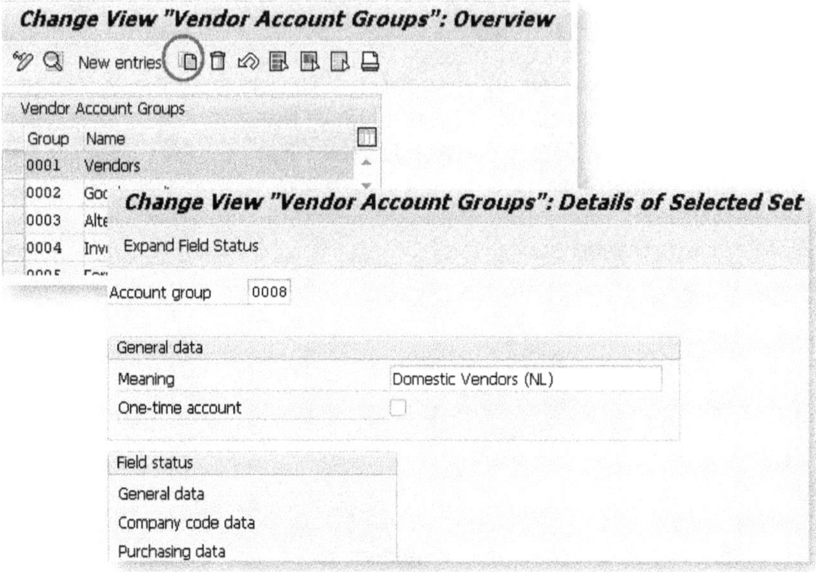

Change View "Vendor Account Groups": Overview

New entries

Vendor Account Groups	
Group	Name
0001	Vendors
0002	Goc
0003	Alte
0004	Inv
0005	For

Change View "Vendor Account Groups": Details of Selected Set

Expand Field Status

Account group   0008

General data	
Meaning	Domestic Vendors (NL)
One-time account	☐

Field status
General data
Company code data
Purchasing data

Figure 5.26: Define vendor account groups

5.6.9   Assign number range to vendor account group

FINANCIAL ACCOUNTING • ACCOUNTS RECEIVABLE AND ACCOUNTS PAYABLE •
VENDOR ACCOUNTS • MASTER DATA • PREPARATIONS FOR CREATING VENDOR
MASTER DATA • ASSIGN NUMBER RANGES TO VENDOR ACCOUNT

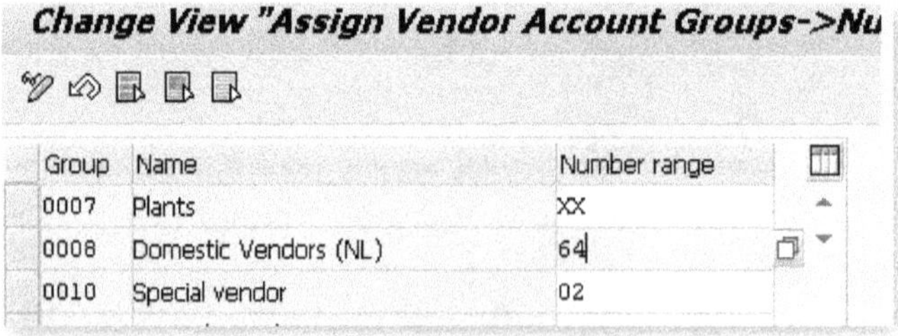

Change View "Assign Vendor Account Groups->Nu

Group	Name	Number range	
0007	Plants	XX	
0008	Domestic Vendors (NL)	64	
0010	Special vendor	02	

Figure 5.27: Assign number range to vendor account group

5.6.10 AP document number ranges

FINANCIAL ACCOUNTING (NEW) • FINANCIAL ACCOUNTING GLOBAL SETTINGS
(NEW) • DOCUMENT • DOCUMENT TYPES • DEFINE DOCUMENT TYPES FOR
ENTRY VIEW (transaction OBA7)

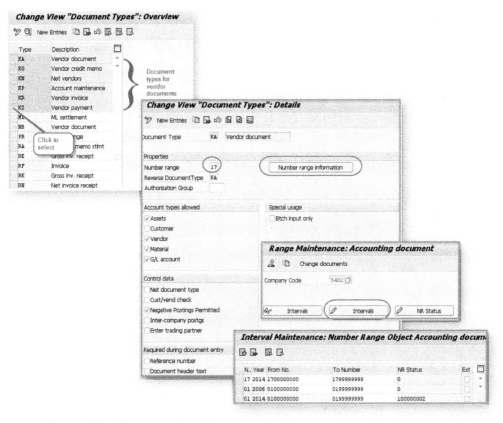

Figure 5.28: AP document number ranges

5.6.11 Account determination for discount and payment differences

Transaction FBKP

Figure 5.29: Account determination for discount and payment differences

You have finished the book.

A About the Author

Ann Cacciottoli is a Specialist Senior with Deloitte, the world's largest private professional services firm. She has over 14 years of experience delivering SAP solutions, with a focus on SAP Financials and Reporting. She currently resides in Godfrey, IL. Her client-service work has taken her to Europe, Asia, and throughout the United States.

Ann has always been very passionate about sharing her knowledge and experience with those new to SAP.

B Index

C Solutions to Exercises

This chapter provides solutions to the exercises in Chapters 1–4.

Solutions for Chapter 1

1.6.1 Log into the IDES client, expand the menu, and answer the following questions

1. List three transaction codes for entering a General Ledger (G/L) account document.

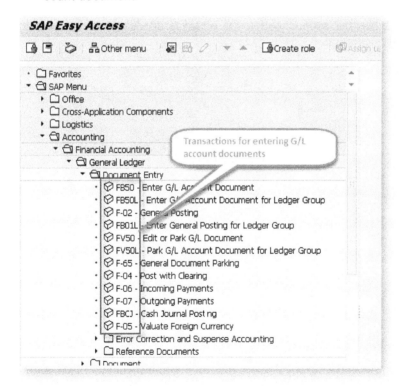

Figure 1: Solution 1.6.1-1

2. List three transaction codes for entering an Accounts Payable (AP) document.

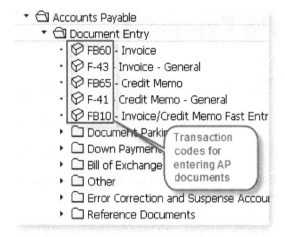

Figure 2: Solution 1.6.1-2

3. List three transaction codes for entering an Accounts Receivable (AR) document.

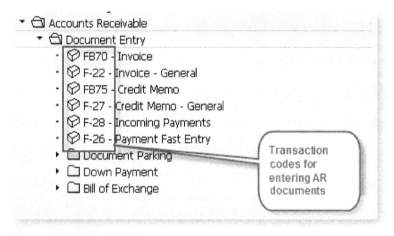

Figure 3: Solution 1.6.1-3

1.6.2 Add transaction FB03 - Display to the Favorites folder

1. Expand the SAP Easy Access menu so that transaction FB03 is displayed:

Figure 4: Solution 1.6.2-1

2. Right-click FB03 and select ADD TO FAVORITES

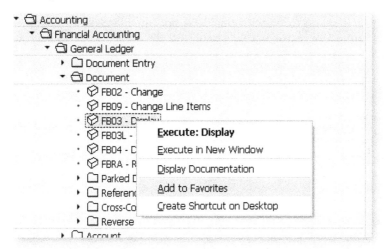

Figure 5: Solution 1.6.2-2

3. Note that the transaction is now located in the Favorites folder.

Figure 6: Solution 1.6.2-3

1.6.3 Navigate to the Enter G/L Account Document screen and exit without creating an entry

1. Expand the menu to transaction FB50 and double-click to select or enter FB50 in the command field and click ✓.

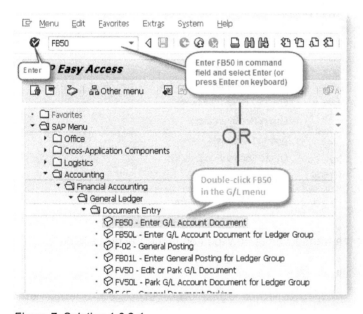

Figure 7: Solution 1.6.3-1

2. Select the CANCEL icon to return to the SAP Easy Access menu

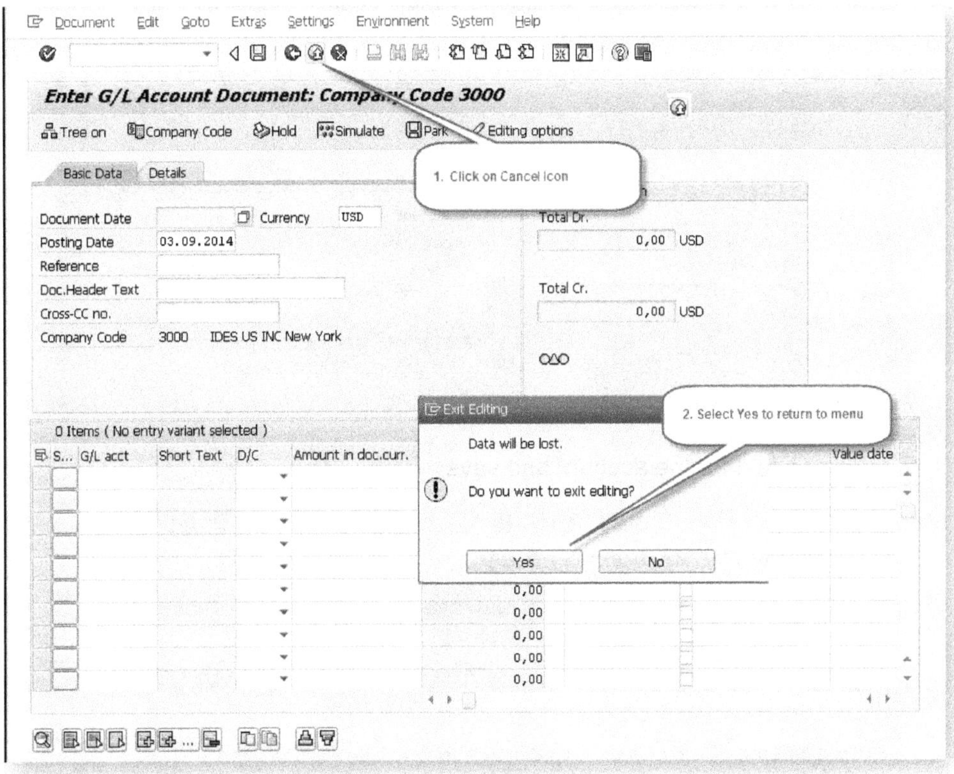

Figure 8: Solution 1.6.3-2

Solutions for Chapter 2

2.4.1 Add a G/L account (expense account)

1. Use transaction FS00 to copy account 474270 to 474272.

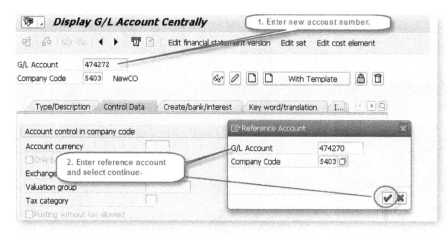

Figure 9: Solution 2.4.1-1

2. Enter a text for the account and save 💾.

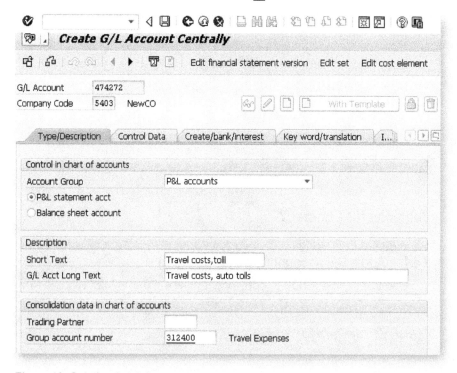

Figure 10: Solution 2.4.1-2

2.4.2 Post an entry to include the new expense account

1. Use transaction FB50 and enter the document information. Click 🖫 to post the entry.

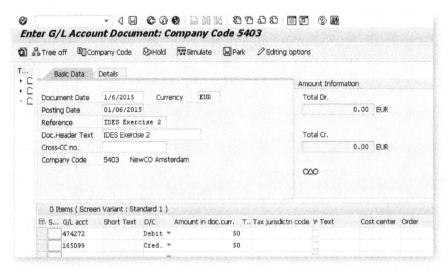

Figure 11: Solution 2.4.2-1

2. Use transaction FB03 to display the document.

Figure 12: Solution 2.4.2-2

2.4.3 Add an open item G/L account

1. Use transaction FS00 to copy account 159100 to 159105.

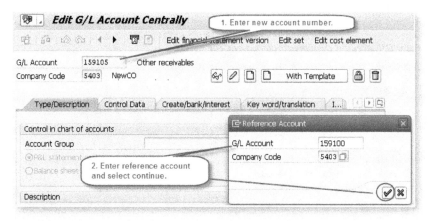

Figure 13: Solution 2.4.3-1

2. Enter a text for the account and click 💾.

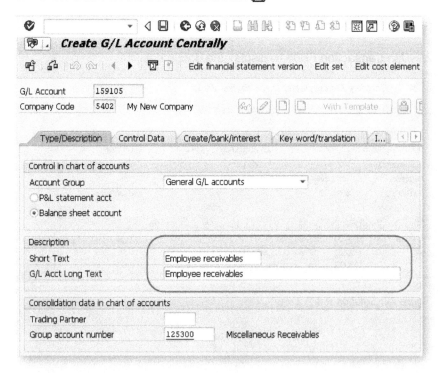

Figure 14: Solution 2.4.3-2

2.4.4 Post an entry to the new open item account

1. Use transaction FB50.

2. Enter details for the entry and click 🖫 to post.

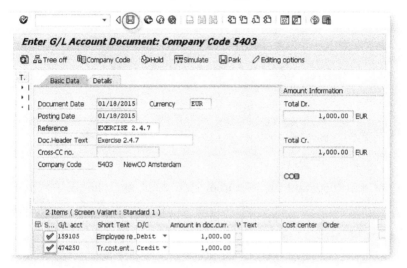

Figure 15: Solution 2.4.4-2

2.4.5 Post with clearing to clear the item posted above.

1. Use transaction F-04.

2. Enter header information for the document and then select CHOOSE OPEN ITEMS.

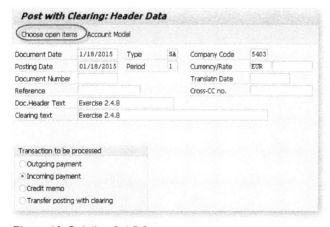

Figure 16: Solution 2.4.5 2

3. Choose DOCUMENT NUMBER and select PROCESS OPEN ITEMS.

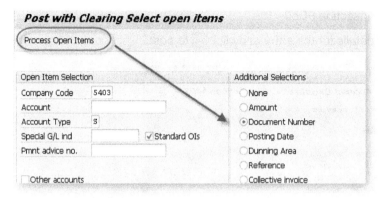

Figure 17: Solution 2.4.5-3

4. Enter the document number from step 2.4.4 and choose PROCESS OPEN ITEMS.

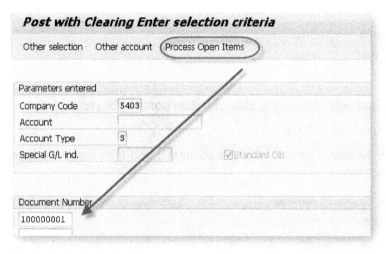

Figure 18: Solution 2.4.5-4

5. Select CHARGE OFF DIFFERENCE.

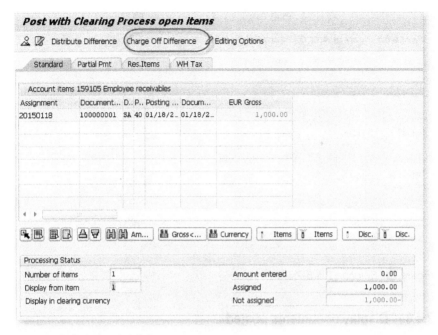

Figure 19: Solution 2.4.5-5

6. Enter posting key 40 and click ✅.

Figure 20: Solution 2.4.5-6

7. Enter an amount and click 🖫 to post the document.

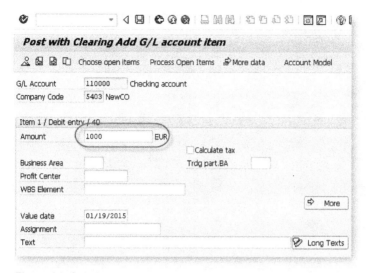

Figure 21: Solution 2.4.5-7

2.4.6 Display documents posted

1. Use transaction FB03.

2. Enter the document number and click ✅ .

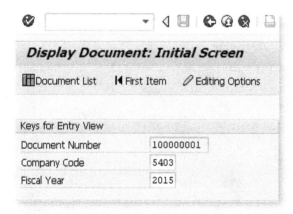

Figure 22: Solution 2.4.6-2

3. Choose the BACK icon and repeat step 2 for the second document.

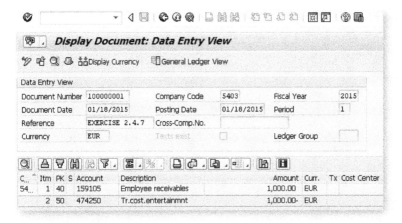

Figure 23: Solution 2.4.6-3

4.   Chose BACK 🌐 to return to menu.

Solutions for Chapter 3

3.5.1   Create a customer

1.   Use transaction FD01. Select the new account group and click ✔ to continue.

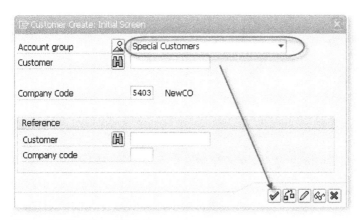

Figure 24: Solution 3.5.1-1

2.   Enter the customer information and then choose COMPANY CODE DATA.

Figure 25: Solution 3.5.1-2

3. Enter the reconciliation account and click 💾.

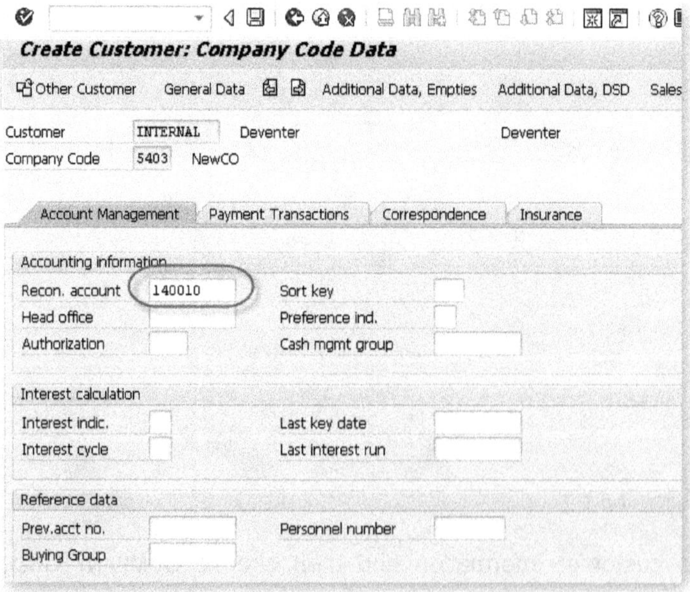

Figure 26: Solution 3.5.1-3

4. Note the message returned with the customer number.

✓ Customer 0050000001 has been created for company code 5403

Figure 27: Solution 3.5.1-4

3.5.2 Post two customer invoices

Use transaction FB70, enter the invoice information, and click 🖫 to post.

Figure 28: Solution 3.5.2, invoice #1

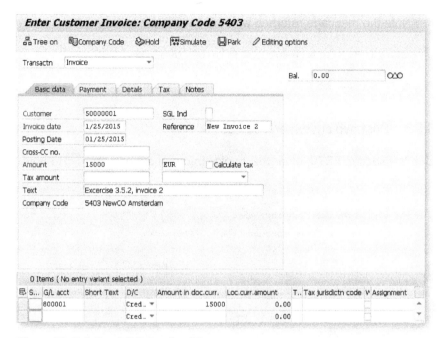

Figure 29: Solution 3.5.2, invoice #2

3.5.3 Post a payment receipt for one of the customer invoices created

1. Execute transaction F-28, enter the document information, and then choose PROCESS OPEN ITEMS.

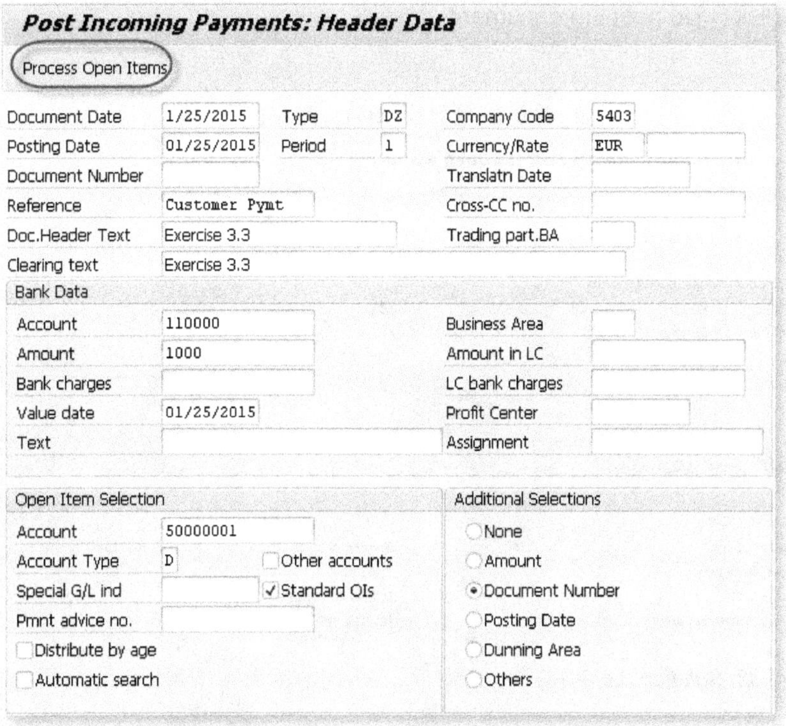

Figure 30: Solution 3.5.3-1

2. Enter the document number to be cleared and choose PROCESS OPEN ITEMS.

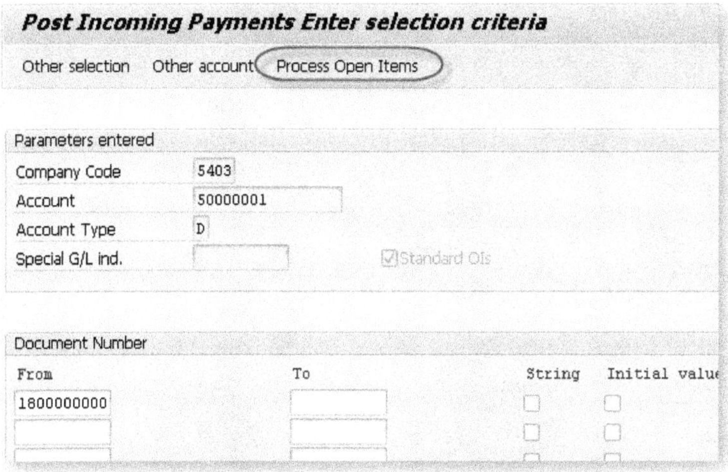

Figure 31 Solution 3.5.3-2

3. Click 🖫 to post the document.

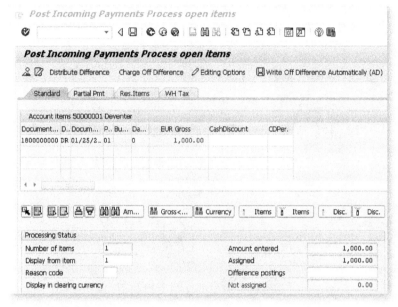

Figure 32: Solution 3.5.3-3

3.5.4 Display open items with standard reports/transaction codes

1. Use transaction FBL5N, enter the customer and company code, select OPEN ITEMS, and click ⊕ to execute.

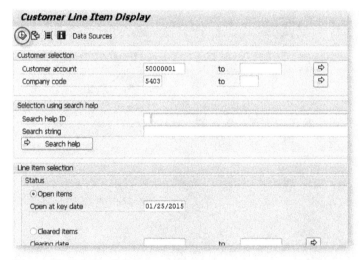

Figure 33: Solution 3.5.4-1

2. Customer line items are displayed. Choose BACK 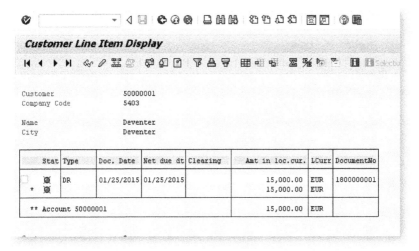 to return to the menu.

Figure 34: Solution 3.5.4-2

Solutions for Chapter 4

4.5.1   Create a vendor

1. Use transaction FK01, select the new account group, and click ✅ .

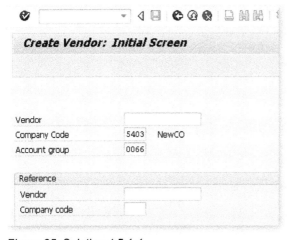

Figure 35: Solution 4.5.1-1

2. Enter the details and then choose the NEXT SCREEN icon ▣ until the ACCOUNTING INFORMATION screen appears.

Figure 36: Solution 4.5.1-2

3. Enter the reconciliation account and click ▣.

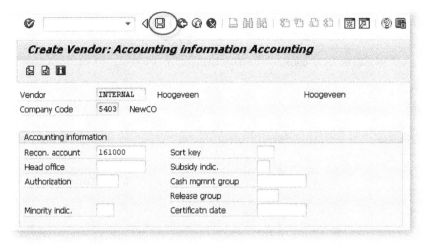

Figure 37: Solution 4.5.1-3

4.5.2 Post a vendor invoice

1. Use transaction FB60, enter the invoice information, and click 🖫 to post the document.

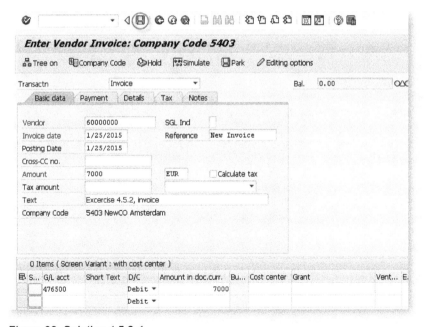

Figure 38: Solution 4.5.2-1

4.5.3 Display line items for the vendor

1. Use transaction FBL1N, enter the vendor and company code, select OPEN ITEMS, and click 🕒 to execute.

Figure 39: Solution 4.5.3-1

2. Vendor line items are displayed. Choose BACK 🔙 to return to the menu.

Figure 40: Solution 4.5.3-2

D Disclaimer

This publication contains references to the products of SAP SE.

SAP, R/3, SAP NetWeaver, Duet, PartnerEdge, ByDesign, SAP BusinessObjects Explorer, StreamWork, and other SAP products and services mentioned herein as well as their respective logos are trademarks or registered trademarks of SAP SE in Germany and other countries.

Business Objects and the Business Objects logo, BusinessObjects, Crystal Reports, Crystal Decisions, Web Intelligence, Xcelsius, and other Business Objects products and services mentioned herein as well as their respective logos are trademarks or registered trademarks of Business Objects Software Ltd. Business Objects is an SAP company.

Sybase and Adaptive Server, iAnywhere, Sybase 365, SQL Anywhere, and other Sybase products and services mentioned herein as well as their respective logos are trademarks or registered trademarks of Sybase, Inc. Sybase is an SAP company.

SAP SE is neither the author nor the publisher of this publication and is not responsible for its content. SAP Group shall not be liable for errors or omissions with respect to the materials. The only warranties for SAP Group products and services are those that are set forth in the express warranty statements accompanying such products and services, if any. Nothing herein should be construed as constituting an additional warranty.

More Espresso Tutorials Books

Martin Munzel & Jörg Siebert:

First Steps in SAP®

- ▶ Learn what SAP and SAP software is all about!
- ▶ Enhanced with videos and audio comments
- ▶ Simple, consecutive examples

http://5014.espresso-tutorials.com/

Dieter Schlagenhauf & Jörg Siebert:

SAP® Fixed Assets Accounting (FI-AA)

- ▶ Processes and Functions in SAP ERP Financials
- ▶ Validation and Reporting for IFRS
- ▶ Posting Examples
- ▶ Periodic Activities Explained

http://5023.espresso-tutorials.com/

Stefan Eifler:

Quick Guide to SAP® CO-PA (Profitability Analysis)

- ▶ Basic organizational entities and master data
- ▶ Define the actual value flow
- ▶ Set up a planning environment
- ▶ Create your own reports

http://5018.espresso-tutorials.com/

Thomas Michael:

Reporting for SAP® Asset Accounting

▶ Basic asset accounting reporting features

▶ Balance, transaction and specialtity reports

▶ Asset history sheet and US tax reporting

http://5029.espresso-tutorials.com

Lennart B. Ullmann & Claus Wild:

Electronic Bank Statement and Lockbox in SAP® ERP

▶ Processing the Electronic Bank Statement in SAP

▶ Integrating Payment Advices as of SAP EhP 5

▶ New Functionality for Post-Processing as of SAP EhP 6

▶ Detailed Message Monitoring and Reprocessing Examples

http:/5056.espresso-tutorials.com/

Tanya Duncan:

Practical Guide to SAP® CO-PC (Product Cost Controlling)

▶ Cost Center Planning Process and Costing Run Execution

▶ Actual Cost Analysis & Reporting

▶ Controlling Master Data

▶ Month End Processes in Details

http://5064.espresso-tutorials.com/

Stephen Birchall:

Invoice Verification for SAP®

▶ Learn everything you need for invoice verification and its role in FI and MM

▶ Keep user input to a minimum and automate the process

▶ Discover best practices to configure and maximize the use of this function

http://5073.espresso-tutorials.com